GROWING YOUR CLIENT BASE

Growing Your Client Base

The step-by-step guide
to business development
in professional services

Paul Denvir and Kevin Walker

PACE

Growing Your Client Base

Published by The PACE Partners LLP
Copyright The PACE Partners LLP 2007

For more information, contact The PACE Partners, PACE House, Churchfield Road, Walton on Thames, Surrey, KT12 2TZ or visit us on the World Wide Web at: http://www.thepacepartners.com

ISBN 978-0-9552273-3-2

First published 2007 by The PACE Partnership

Contents

Introduction

Over the past ten years we at PACE have focused our energies on working with professional services firms with a view to assisting them in the areas of leadership, client relationship management and new business development. It has to be said that professional firms in general have made great strides in these areas within the last decade. The standards have improved immeasurably and there have been a number of reasons for this.

Firstly clients have become more demanding of their advisors, not only in respect of the services that advisors provide but also in relation to the way they expect these firms to run themselves. This has caused professional firms to look more closely at their governance and leadership, at the way in which they manage client relationships and the way that they market and sell. Increased competition has further sharpened this focus.

Secondly firms have been more open to employing people (particularly in the marketing function) who have come from other industries. These appointments have not been universally successful. Too often there has been a mismatch of expectation from both sides and the relationship has been both uncomfortable and short. However, some of the marketers brought into professional services firms have worked hard and have successfully made the transition. They have approached the professions with an open mind and not a desire to superimpose their earlier learning and experiences gained in another market sector. Having learned how the professional services marketplace works these people have then been able to take their expertise and apply it in way that is in concert with the way that professional firms operate.

This has led to the existence of the third factor that has assisted firms in making the strides that they have. Today in the UK there is a hard core of very savvy marketing and business development professionals who really understand what needs to be done in order to grow the franchise of a professional firm. These people have helped their firms to become more commercially minded and more professional in their approach to the market.

These people sometimes struggle to make the impact that they would ideally desire. Trying to work with a business full of engineers, lawyers, actuaries, property consultants or accountants is not easy particularly when these people's main agenda is usually the execution of fee-earning work.

Whilst generally speaking there has been significant progress within professional services firms in the way they approach new business development, this progress is not universal. There are firms – and sometimes practice areas or market facing groups within firms – that are exemplars of best practice and are therefore very successful in new business acquisition. On the other hand there are firms, and parts of firms, that have a very long way to go in respect of the way they manage business development.

This book is written with a number of different people in mind. It is aimed at:

Managing partners and marketing partners

We believe that we have captured pragmatic best practice. You can benchmark the marketing and business development activities that are carried out within your firm against this best practice.

Business unit heads – practice area leaders or market facing group heads

You don't have to wait for the whole of the firm to decide how it will go about its business development activities. You can get started right away. This book will provide you with the framework for what needs to be done.

Marketers new to professional services

The book will provide a structured guide to marketing and selling professional services, which will also allow you to see where your previous knowledge, skills and experience fit.

Experienced professional services marketers

Hopefully this will be another tool that will confirm that your efforts, which sometimes are not fully appreciated, are being aimed in the right direction.

Individual practitioners within professional firms

In writing the book we have drawn on our experiences of working with dozens of firms in all of the professions. Most of our clients are rightly interested mainly in successful implementation. They do not want high-flown theory. They want practical, pragmatic ways of working that will increase their success in business development in increasingly competitive markets. In this publication we have distilled the practices and processes that our clients tell us work. Some of the ideas in the book are ours, some we jointly developed with clients and some we learned directly from clients.

At the completion of each chapter we have included a section on 'Where to go from here'. This section is a summary of some of the actions that could be taken by either people running a firm, people running a business unit within a firm or by individual practitioners to implement some of the ideas contained in the preceding chapter.

Sitting behind the implementable ideas that we share in this book however, are some fundamental beliefs.

- We believe that any business only thrives in the long term if it delivers a distinctive value to its clients.

- We believe that just as a client has a choice as to which firm she will use, so does a professional firm have a choice over which clients it wishes to work with. We believe that the best firms choose the best clients.

- We believe that firms that attract clients like magnets do so because they have built a distinctive reputation. This reputation is created by narrowing the focus of the firm and working to become famous in a small number of areas.

We also believe that a firm can ignore all of these beliefs and still make money but it will never be a great firm – just a firm that is content to be a part of the mediocre – engaging with average clients and attracting average people to work in its business.

In this publication we have focused our attentions on the processes and practices of business development. Other than referring to them in passing we have not attempted to address the associated skills issues in any depth. These are much more extensively covered in one of our other books – *Creating New Clients*.

At the risk of being seen as politically incorrect, and purely for reasons of simplicity throughout this book we will refer to all professionals as being of male gender and all client personnel as being of female gender.

We trust that you will find this book of value.

Acknowledgements

As a publication such as this starts to take on its final shape, it is all too easy for the authors to slip into a mindset – believing that the content is 'theirs'. Indeed, we have learned much through our personal experiences gained whilst carrying out consulting and training assignments with professional services firms, and hopefully this learning and experience is reflected in the way we have tackled this subject.

However, we also recognise and appreciate the contribution made through the experiences, ideas and inputs from colleagues. These have helped shape this publication. In particular we would like to thank Michelle Gahagan, Romey Ghadially, Paul Matthews, John Monks, Susan O'Gorman, Tim Rusling, Paul Telfer, David Tovey, Gary Williams and Paul Wong, all of whom are colleagues from within PACE, for their contribution and encouragement.

Chapter 1   **The PACE Pipeline**

[Note: Readers who are familiar with our earlier publication, *Creating New Clients*, may prefer to skip this chapter, which is an amended version of Chapter One of that book. For those readers new to our thinking, this chapter will introduce the essential framework that holds the ideas in this book together.]

The PACE Pipeline is a tool that enables a firm to have a clear picture of its business development processes and practice. Adoption and application of The PACE Pipeline model brings certainty to a firm's business development efforts. Firms that use the model can plan more accurately the marketing and business development activities they need to carry out and can then analyse the effect of these plans in a structured way. A whole firm can adopt the model or specific practice areas or market facing groups within a firm can apply it. It can even be used by individual fee-earners.

So, what is The PACE Pipeline?

The PACE Pipeline is a tool for the effective project management of business development in professional services firms.

Professional firms today have, in the main, reasonable systems that tell them about the current financial health of the organisation. They know what they have billed, they know what work in progress is still to be billed and they know the work they have booked that they have yet to commence. Too often that is where the measurement and management of fee-earning work finishes. The systems measure the here and now but do nothing about reassuring (or warning) management about the health of future income streams.

The PACE Pipeline and pipeline management are all about ensuring that future fee income is both secure and profitable. In our parlance a practice area that has a strong pipeline would be very certain that future business flow (perhaps three, six or twelve months into the future) was going to be healthy because it had created opportunities that it would be able to convert into future work. People within the practice area – carrying out specific, planned and targeted activities with the firm's clients and prospective clients – have created these opportunities.

The PACE Pipeline is the foundation for the successful management of business development activities.

The model has particular relevance for business development scenarios where the following conditions are typical:

1   It is hard (or impossible) to guarantee the level of future sales (fee) income.

2   There is a time lag between activities put into business development and billable results being produced from this activity.

3   Not all business development activity produces results.

4   It is possible to measure (and manage) business development activity.

We would suggest that these criteria all apply in great measure to the selling of professional services.

On the first point, it is a brave individual who guarantees the fee income he will produce next year. Sometimes it takes courage to take a stab at the fee income projection for next month!

Secondly, there is certainly a time lag between activity put into business development (particularly new client acquisition) and the ensuing results. Non-clients have relationships with other people at other firms. It may take months or years to break these loyalty ties and win a first piece of work.

Related to the third point, all professionals are only too aware that not every effort directed toward business development reaches a successful conclusion. As someone once expressed it to us, "You have to kiss a lot of frogs before you find a prince."

Finally business development activity can be measured. The fact that most firms have poor processes for doing so does not get us away from the fact that this activity can be measured. And what can be measured can be managed.

If a firm's pipeline building activities are well managed then it can be assured of the fee income streams that will guarantee a healthy future. To identify exactly what these activities are we should refer to the model.

THE SEGMENTS OF THE MODEL

There are six parts to The PACE Pipeline model, five lying within the model and one outside. The five parts that lie within are known collectively as the Total Defined Market. Whether client or prospective client these parts of the pipeline are known and defined. Outside the model lie a firm's undefined prospects.

P0 – Undefined Prospects

Outside the perimeter of the model exists the overall market. Within this market there are thousands of organisations that potentially could become clients of the firm. Some we would welcome, some would be a poor fit.

P1 – Defined Prospects not yet marketed to

From the overall marketplace a firm has to make choices as to which prospective clients it would ideally like to work with in the future. Having initially made the choice, there may be a period of time before the firm begins its marketing and business development activities directed toward these organisations.

P2 – Defined Prospects marketed to – not yet in dialogue

Having identified its Defined Prospects a firm then has to begin the process of making the prospect aware of its existence and what it does. Ideally it also tries to convince the client that it is particularly adept in its particular field – perhaps better than the advisors they are using today. Marketing tools and activities are employed to achieve these aims. The objective is to encourage the Defined Prospect to welcome the opportunity to discuss the possibility of working with the firm.

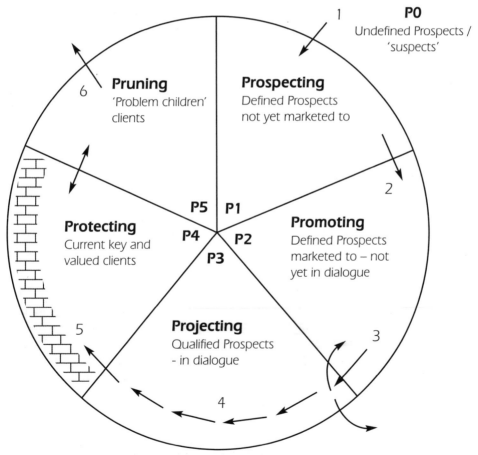

Total Defined Market

P3 – Qualified Prospects

Having created the opportunity to cross the threshold of the Defined Prospect's premises in order to talk business, some of these prospective clients will have a genuine opportunity that is within the remit and capabilities of the firm making the approach. When there is real opportunity that has been qualified as 'winnable' then our Defined Prospect has turned into a Qualified Prospect.

P4 – Current key and valued clients

The successful pursuit of an opportunity identified within a Qualified Prospect leads to the acquisition of a client. In the fullness of time this client may qualify to be recognised as one of the firm's key clients. If not a key client then the client is categorised as one of the firm's valued clients. The distinction between key clients and valued clients – and how a firm may decide how to segment its client base – is covered in some depth in our book *Managing Key Clients*.

P5 – 'Problem children' clients

Every firm has them. Some have more than others. Some have their client base largely built on 'problem children'. These are clients that, in their current state, probably cause the firm more grief than the fee income is worth.

Each of the segments of The PACE Pipeline has a title that reflects the main activity that is occurring at each stage of the pipeline building process – Prospecting, Promoting, Projecting (that we will win work at some point in the future), Protecting and (potentially) Pruning.

PIPELINE BUILDING ACTIVITY

The arrows on The PACE Pipeline model represent the activities in which a firm has to engage in order to build its pipeline of future business. In sequence the activities are as follows.

Arrow 1

This is the work that has to be carried out in order that the firm can accurately identify those organisations in the marketplace that it wishes to do business with at some point in the future. Success in this activity produces a clearly agreed list of Defined Prospects. This list is compiled through the application of relevant selection criteria to prospective clients in the overall (P0) marketplace. How a firm goes about this process is the subject of Chapter 2.

Arrow 2

This is the marketing activity that is directed towards Defined Prospects. There are a plethora of marketing tools and activities available to a professional services firm. It is critical that firms understand the potential effect of each of the marketing tools available and know how to apply them successfully. This is the focus of Chapter 3.

Arrow(s) 3

The result of excellent marketing activity directed toward prospective clients is a ringing telephone – the Defined Prospect calling us and telling us that they would like to talk with someone from our firm. In an ideal world this would happen all the time. In the real world it only happens some of the time. When it doesn't happen then fee-earners within the firm have to be prepared, when the timing is right, to pick up the telephone and make proactive verbal contact with people within the Defined Prospect organisation with a view to agreeing a meeting. This is not about cold calling. We refer to this process in Chapters 3 and 4 and cover the skills element of telephoning for appointments quite extensively in our book *Creating New Clients*. In the ideal world a first meeting with a Defined Prospect would always result in:

- Our image of the Defined Prospect as a desirable future client even more enhanced by the conclusion of the meeting.

- The identification of a real opportunity that we are interested in pursuing and the client is interested in discussing further with us.

Back in the real world neither of these ideal scenarios occur every time. Our cluster of arrows at action stage 3 shows three possibilities. The best outcome is the straight arrow. We proceed to the fourth set of arrows in the business development process.

However, in the course of an initial meeting we may uncover any number of facts that lead us to other conclusions. As much as the prospect may have looked interesting from our initial due diligence back at the arrow 1 stage, in fact there may be very good reasons why at this point we do not wish to pursue them any further. As shallow and superficial as it may sound, we have walked into reception areas of prospects and before we have started the first meeting we have recognised that the business whose representative we are due to meet with will probably not fit as one of our chosen clients. This interim conclusion is based on evidence that is visual and verbal. The following hour allows time for gathering more evidence on which to make a final decision. If, based on first-hand experience, the prospect is unsuitable we should not pursue the contact further but rather return the organisation back to the P0 'pool'.

More common is the arrow that returns the Defined Prospect to the P2 Promoting segment of the pipeline.

In this instance we finish the meeting still convinced that the Defined Prospect is the sort of organisation that we would like to have as a client someday, but with no specific opportunity having been agreed between the two parties that would provide the basis for immediate on-going dialogue. In this situation the Defined Prospect should then continue to be targeted through our marketing. The fact that we did not find an immediate opportunity at the first meeting does not mean that everything that went before was wrong. It simply means that our timing was out.

We have to ensure that when a potential opportunity does occur in the future that we are far enough to the front of the Defined Prospect's mind that they include us in their thinking. As Woody Allen said in one of his movies, "80% of success is showing up." We have to continue to 'show up' by using our marketing tools and by keeping in contact via e-mail and the telephone.

Professional firms in general are poor at maintaining this sort of on-going contact. Fee-earners conclude that there is nothing much to be won from the prospective client and whilst there is an initial intention to keep contact, this lapses quickly as the professional becomes engaged in other priorities – mostly fee-earning work. The real damage of this behaviour is only experienced some time – maybe months or years – later when a colleague contacts the prospective client again to hear: "I don't know why you're contacting us again. One of your people was here about a year ago. Made all sorts of promises to keep in touch but we never heard from him again. We concluded that you obviously weren't interested in our business. We've gone elsewhere in the meantime and are very happy with the service we're getting."

Arrow(s) 4

These arrows represent the management and execution of the selling activity that turns an identified opportunity within a Qualified Prospect into a piece of work. The practices, tools and tactics for successfully managing the sales process are detailed in Chapter 4. We examine more of the skills employed in this phase of the business development process in our book *Creating New Clients*.

Brickwall 5

The activity here is represented by the image of the brick wall. The aim is to build relationships with key and valued clients to the point that it is unlikely that they will defect to our competitors. This is a huge subject that we will not attempt to cover in this publication. We have though, dedicated a whole book *Managing Key Clients*, to this subject. One subset of brickwalling activity that we will examine in some detail in this book, *Managing Business Development*, is the business development issue of cross-selling. Chapter 5 is devoted to this subject.

Arrow 6

If a client has drifted into being a 'problem child', the question is what are we going to do about it? In Chapter 6 we look at the issues that can cause a client to be regarded as a 'problem child' and also examine the actions that can be taken.

TRAPS IN PIPELINE MANAGEMENT

We continually see two common problems that stem from a lack of detailed management of the Pipeline. These problems result in the firm, practice area or individual experiencing the roller coaster ride of 'feast and famine'. The problems are so endemic that many professionals come to the conclusion that big swings in business levels are impossible to avoid. Fortunately this is not true – if we avoid the following traps then we will avoid the dangerous implications of the 'feast and famine' cycle.

Trap 1 The implications of the mix of activity are not considered

Take the case of a team who, when examining their Pipeline for the next year, come to the conclusion that their objectives can be met by working with their existing clients plus bringing on board four big new clients. When the team looks at its P3 Projecting segment it finds that it has six major prospects which have distinct possibilities of being converted within the next year.

The team puts all its efforts into converting these opportunities. The selling and contact campaigns are worked out and co-ordinated and everyone puts in maximum effort. By the second half of the year, four have been won and it is clear that in the other two cases there is no prospect of winning work in the short term. Two out of three ain't bad. The question is, from where will the new business come in Year 2?

Twelve months on when the team is considering its business development plans for Year 2, it is looking at an empty P3 segment. The team also recognises one of the underpinning principles of the pipeline concept – that there is a time lag between activities being devoted to business development and the results of that effort. Twelve months may not be long enough to bring prospects through from the P2 segment to becoming clients. Even if the team could be successful in this task, success will probably happen towards the end of Year 2 and will have little impact on Year 2 income.

Again, this scenario is working on the assumption that the team has a healthy P2 segment – lots of interesting looking Defined Prospects who have been kept warm through good marketing efforts. Did that happen in Year 1 or was that one of the casualties of the big push to convert the six?

During Year 1 when the big push was under way, was effort also put into updating the quality and quantity of prospects considered 'Defined' – as a feeder for the P2 segment?

There needs to be a balance of activity put into the different segments of the Pipeline if we are to control the flow of business in both the short and long term. There is no standard formula that can be applied. Each firm needs to consider its situation and decide how that balance of activity should be apportioned.

Some activity needs to be exerted into all segments of the Pipeline. The firm then has to ensure that individuals are responsible and accountable for those activities which will generate the business flow which the organisation requires.

Trap 2   People become victims of their own success - too busy or too complacent

This is an all too common situation. The diagram below depicts what happens. Let us take the scenario of a professional given the responsibility and a clear field to develop new business. The horizontal axis represents time. The vertical axis measures the level of activity and the level of results.

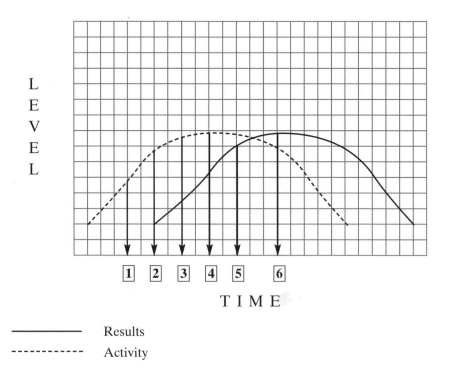

| ——————— | Results |
| ------------- | Activity |

For a period of time the professional puts in effort and produces no results. (Timeline Point 1.) This is the Pipeline time-lag principle manifesting itself again.

In this scenario the level of effort put into selling and marketing then increases quite sharply. Perhaps the person has completed some professional work and more of his effort is business development orientated, perhaps he is concerned with a lack of early success and decides to work even harder. There could be a number of factors influencing this increase in activity.

However, if we look at the Timeline Point 2, the results are disappointing. Most people in the firm will only be aware of this aspect of the campaign. After all, the systems only measure results. It could even be at this point that someone senior decides to 'pull the plug'. There have been many months of effort and very little success to show for it.

At Timeline Point 3 we see some reasonable results coming through and the effort is very high. At Timeline Point 4 the results are definitely looking good and the activity has peaked. At this point in time the professional has generated an extremely good flow of work but he is working 14 hours a day, six days a week on his quest. This cannot continue and it is only natural that the activity dips from this peak.

At Timeline Point 5 the activity has clearly dropped but interestingly the results continue to climb. One particular reason for this phenomenon is very common to professional services firms. Fee-earners are most often not only responsible for generating the income but are also involved in the design and delivery of the 'product'. The more work won, the less time there is for marketing and business development.

At Timeline Point 6, results are at their zenith but business development activity has dropped away considerably. This effort level has no immediate impact on business levels – but it will. The only question is when.

So what should the professional do at Timeline Point 6? He could work harder, reduce his own chargeable work or recruit more resources and through these efforts build up his selling activity to generate more opportunities. However, even if he were to do this the results of this second wave of activity may not generate business before the results curve dips alarmingly. The time to redirect activity is at Timeline Point 3 or 4, on the basis of the projection of future business (the pipeline) not past results. In fact Timeline Point 6 is the worst time to recruit new resources – i.e. in advance of a dip in business. We may be recruiting for redundancy.

The trap occurs because, as we pointed out at the very beginning of this chapter, the measurements that most firms have in place only relate to the results curve, therefore decisions are made on this information. Remember – results can lie! The key is to make the dotted line visible and manage it well – i.e. manage the Pipeline as well as the results it brings.

USING THE PACE PIPELINE MODEL

We see increasingly that our clients use The PACE Pipeline as the basis for managing their marketing and business development activities. They find that the model is simple but at the same time is comprehensive. They also find that it introduces a common language across the firm. When someone says, "We've got a strong P4 pipeline but our P3 is looking really thin. We need to look at our P2 prospects and see if we can advance them more quickly in some way", then everyone grasps the issue immediately.

It is gratifying to walk into practice areas or market facing groups and to see the team's Pipeline shown graphically using flip chart sheets on the wall. People can physically follow the progression of the team's prospects as they move closer to becoming clients. We have some clients who have reconfigured their databases so that the P status of all entries is a key piece of information. In that way the firm can take a snapshot from any number of angles as to the structure of their Pipeline – by practice area, by office or by individual.

Being such a visual tool facilitates easy sharing of information. This enables marketing and business development people to be 'on the same page' as their fee-earning colleagues – in turn helping to generate commitment to common goals.

Also The PACE Pipeline maps out a process. Because of this we find that fee-earners relate to the model well as most of their roles are based around the application of well-proven, sturdy processes.

The PACE Pipeline is the foundation for the successful management of business development activities.

WHERE TO GO FROM HERE

Where to go from here if you run a firm or have overall responsibility for marketing and business development

Look at the way the firm manages its marketing and business development. Is there a clear, consistent and cogent model that underpins these activities? If the answer is no, then consider introducing The PACE Pipeline as a tool and process to bring focus, clarity and commonality of language to your business.

Ask whether there are any current ways that business development activity (which is the source of all new work) is measured within your firm. If it is poorly measured then it must be poorly managed. Get a group of interested parties together and make them responsible for creating a way to measure business activity within your organisation.

Where to go from here if you run a business unit within a professional firm

Take all of the clients and prospective clients that your business unit has contact with and drop them into the five segments of The PACE Pipeline. What does this picture tell you with regard to the marketing and business development activities that you need to focus on in the future?

Consider a wall display that shows visually to everyone in the business unit what the department's Pipeline looks like.

If you are not doing so today, then begin measuring the Pipeline building activity that your department or group carries out.

Where to go from here if you are a marketing or business development professional working with fee-earners

Introduce The PACE Pipeline to the fee-earners that you work with. Professionals are typically looking for a model that explains simply and clearly a subject that they often find fuzzy and unclear.

Use The PACE Pipeline model in your discussions with the firm's management with regard to where your (and your department's) priorities should lie – and your activities be focused – over the next few months or year.

Where to go from here if you are an individual practitioner within a professional firm

Take all of your clients and prospective clients and drop them into The PACE Pipeline model. What does this tell you about the marketing and business development activities that you need to engage in to build your pipeline of future work?

Use your conclusions from this first exercise as the basis of a discussion with the marketing and business development support people that you have within your firm. How can they support and supplement your efforts?

Chapter 2 **Prospecting**

A simple way to begin thinking about how to carry out activity arrow number one on The PACE Pipeline model is to ask, "If, in three years time we were to have a 'designer' client base, what would it look like? What sort of organisations would populate our ideal P4 segment?" The aim is to create this client base of the future.

NARROW THE FOCUS

As David Peoples in his book *Selling to the Top* said, "If you try to be everything to everybody then you will be nothing to nobody." The firms that we see as being most successful in the management of new business development have a very clear perspective of the markets in which their prospective new clients operate. Moreover they tend to organise themselves along market facing lines rather than along practice area lines.

It is easy to understand why professional firms organise themselves first and foremost along practice lines. It makes firm governance much easier.

However that cuts little ice with clients and prospective clients. One of the demands that virtually all clients have of their advisors is that they expect them to understand their business and the market in which they operate. In the past auditors have said to us, "An audit is an audit. It doesn't matter whether it's a retail business or a haulage company. The principles are exactly the same." Whether or not this argument is factually correct matters not in the slightest. What matters is the client's perception. Most clients want to talk with people whom they believe have a deep understanding of their business.

Imagine for a minute that people in your firm had no need to prospect for new clients, that the telephone was ringing regularly with people who wanted to talk with you and your colleagues about potentially carrying out work for them. Now why would this happen? The most obvious reason would be that your firm has a distinctive reputation. It would be well known for something, perhaps even famous. Yet in legal directories, for instance, one sees even quite small firms that claim to be 'full service' and list almost every imaginable market sector as the areas in which they have expertise. In trying to cover every option these firms are indistinguishable from dozens of others who all make similar claims about the width of their capabilities and their market sector experience.

If a firm wants to stand out and make itself attractive to a sector of the market then it has to decide what sector(s) of the market it wishes to focus upon. Very often this will not mean beginning from scratch. In many firms there is already a weighting toward certain types of clients. These clients may be in financial services, in the not for profit (charities) sector, in the utilities sector, in the public sector or in any other subset of the marketplace. In the case of our own business the sector was professional services.

Worrying about the 'too many eggs in one basket' concern causes firms to 'spread their risk' and to try to win work in new business sectors where they have little expertise and no reputation. This is not a smart way to market. The aim should be to build on strength and focus more of the firm's business development activity into a small number of market sectors where ability is proven and a reputation is at least partially built.

SELECTION CRITERIA – FILTERS AND TRIGGERS

An exercise that we carry out on our Managing Business Development workshops involves the use of two flipcharts. They look as below.

What factors could indicate that a prospective client could be:
More attractive / less attractive
Easier / more difficult to approach?

> What factors could indicate that it may be timely and
> appropriate to approach a prospective client?

We then ask the assembled participants for their suggestions as to what factors could populate each of the sheets. A typical output appears below:

On the first flipchart we have examples of selection criteria that we refer to as filter factors. The positive presence of a number of these factors motivates us to want to win work from a prospective client and we perceive the prospect as being approachable. Who wouldn't want to pursue a prospect where we know they spend lots of money on our kind of capabilities, where we have an excellent track record and where we know the managing director from a previous client relationship?

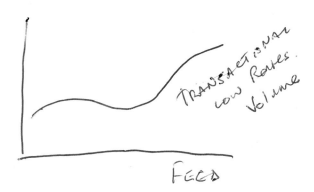

SLA
MSA

> What factors could indicate that a prospective client could be:
>
> More attractive / less attractive
>
> Easier / more difficult to approach?
>
> Prospect has a track record of utilising our kind of services
>
> Prospect has limited internal capability
>
> Prospect is neither too sophisticated for our kind of capabilities nor too unsophisticated
>
> We believe that there could be a good cultural fit ✗
>
> ✓ The prospect spends a lot of money on our kinds of capabilities *EXTERNAL*
>
> ✓ The prospect is in a market sector that we understand and where we have a strong track record
>
> ✓ The work that the prospect gives out is appealing to us *core business*
>
> ✓ We know people within the prospect with whom we can gain entry ——
>
> We know people outside the prospect who can introduce us into the organisation
>
> ✗ The size of the prospect in relation to our firm and our ideal client
>
> ✓ The geographical location of the prospect
>
> The image of the prospect – lack of probity issues
>
> The (lack of) possibility of conflicts

On the second flipchart we have examples of selection criteria that we call trigger factors. On the assumption that there is work to be won within a prospective client, if we have a number of filter factors in our favour then we have probably identified a good prospect. However this does rely on that assumption – that there is work for new advisors and that hopefully this work is plentiful.

The presence of one or more appropriate trigger factors means that there will probably be work for professional firms. Triggers are all about change. Very often this is change over which the prospective client has no control – such as changes in their marketplace or changes in legislation. It is a fact that when most organisations face change they do not possess all of the expertise internally to deal with this change. They need to employ external advisors to assist.

What factors could indicate that it may be timely and appropriate to approach a prospective client?

New MSA

Change in senior management ✔

Deterioration in relationship with current advisors ✔

Change of incumbent's relationship partner

Impending reorganisation

Relocation

Potential acquisition or merger

Potential MBO / MBI

Decision of prospect to enter new markets / business area ✔

New legislation / regulation affecting prospect ✔

Change in business fortune – downturn or sudden increase

Appropriateness of incumbent advisors to prospect's current situation

Major new capital acquisition ✔

Change in prospect's market conditions e.g. new competition or new technology

In the early years of the twenty first century professional firms have suffered from (sometimes substantial) fee income reductions as a result of a severe downturn in one form of trigger event – the merger or acquisition. Acquisitions require merchant bankers, lawyers and accountants. Properties need to be valued so there is work for the property consultants. Pension funds need to be restructured and so the actuaries find gainful employment. Then once the acquisition or merger has taken place the new organisation has to be built. Enter the HR and IT consultants and a raft of other advisors.

Yes, mergers and acquisitions are good news for most professional services businesses. They are an excellent trigger and therefore we may, for instance, wish to consider a prospective client's merger and acquisition track record as a trigger factor.

This may provide an indication to the likelihood of us knocking on a prospect's door at around the time there is work to be won.

However firms, practice areas and market facing groups that have experience in using filter and trigger selection criteria do not just take one criterion in isolation. They use a basket of factors – looking at a number of both types of selection criteria. To start the process of isolating the Defined Prospects that we wish to populate our P1, Prospecting segment with, we have found in practice that it is usually much more practical to begin by selecting a number of filter factors. As our clients have remarked to us over the years, the trigger factors are very powerful but it may take a lot of research to find out if a particular prospective client is 'trigger rich'. And what is the use of all the effort involved in coming to that happy conclusion to then decide that the geographical location of the prospect's offices makes the whole pursuit very unattractive?

Applying Filter and Trigger Selection Criteria

A while back we were working with the facilities management (FM) practice of a large consulting engineering practice. The FM business had a good track record in the public sector and some expertise in certain parts of the private sector. The management of this business had been given the mandate by the parent company to grow the FM business substantially. The growth was to come from the private sector. Like many firms this business had no dedicated sales and marketing resource. Three professionals, who also had other roles to fulfil, were mainly responsible for the business development effort. Being so resource constrained the firm had to target its selling efforts very carefully and so they put in place a set of selection criteria that would help them with the choice of the businesses that they wished to target.

Their application of filters and triggers selection criteria is shown on the next page.

The first two filter factors were quite easy to determine. What experience did the firm have in the prospect's market sector and how good a match was there between the location of the prospect's properties and the siting of the firm's main support centres? If the match was very good, then the prospect would be scored five points (right hand column). If the match was reasonable then the prospect would score two points (middle column) and if the match was poor the prospect would attract no points (left hand column).

The third filter took a bit of desk research. How financially resilient was the prospect? This was a 'default' filter. A prospect had to score five points or it was automatically eliminated at this point. This factor was the only default criterion that the firm used in its selection criteria. The fourth filter factor involved an estimate of the level of income that could be derived from the prospect. By knowing the size, type and location of the property portfolio a rough calculation could be made. Clearly the greater the income potential the more interesting the prospect looked to the FM business.

Having examined potential prospects through the lens of the filter factors, the business then took the best scoring organisations through examination against a number of trigger factors. Had there been a merger or acquisition in the recent past where the business was still looking for economies? Was the business growing quickly – and therefore wanting to devote its energies to its core business? How did the City see the

Example of application of filters and triggers selection criteria – facilities management business

Selection Criteria	Value		
	0	**2**	**5**
Our sector expertise	None	Little / some	Substantial
Geographical match of premises with our centres	Poor	→	Very good
Financial resilience	xxxxxxxxxxxxxxx	xxxxxxxxxxxxxxx	Strong / viable
Potential income per annum	< £250K	→	> £2 million
Merger / acquisition	No	In past	Recent
Growth of business	Static	→	Very fast
City pressures	Viewed as performing well	→	Seen as underperforming. Under pressure
Key personnel changes	None	→	New MD / FD

MSA — t

Triggers

business – was it critical of its profitability? Had there been any changes in senior personnel in the reasonably recent past – were there any new brooms looking to sweep clean? This is a good example of the practical implementation of selection criteria for the following reasons.

• All the criteria were very relevant to the business concerned and were selected by the people who would be involved in the new business acquisition programme.

- There were a good number of criteria used (eight) which made the process quite robust. At the same time not too many were used, which would have made the selection process very prolonged and time consuming.
- There was a good mix of both filter factors and trigger factors with just one default criterion included (financial resilience).

It was gratifying to maintain contact with the management team of this business during the next couple of years. The organisations they directed their marketing toward and followed up with were those that scored most highly against their selection criteria. The businesses that they engaged in initial discussions were of course these same entities and the new clients that came on board in the next eighteen months to two years were, inevitably, the Defined Prospects that they had chosen at the outset.

To create a 'designer' client base a firm, practice area or market facing group has to firstly set out the criteria that determine the most attractive prospective clients for the capabilities and value proposition that it brings to the market. Secondly it must devote the energy and activity to scan the potential market through the lens of these criteria in order to arrive at its set of Defined Prospects. This is activity arrow one of The PACE Pipeline.

Defined Prospects and Key Defined Prospects

We usually find that when a firm goes through the process of using selection criteria to determine its most interesting Defined Prospects, that the sifting process produces three 'grades' of output.

Firstly there are very often a large number of prospects that are not brought into the P1 Prospecting segment of The PACE Pipeline. They don't make the cut and remain as 'undefined prospects' – usually for a combination of reasons.

At the other end of the spectrum there are a fairly small number of highly exciting Defined Prospects. There is a very strong correlation between these organisations and most of our selection criteria. These are our Key Defined Prospects.

The group in the middle are interesting Defined Prospects – not quite as exciting as the 'top set' Key Defined Prospects – but definitely worth winning work from. The total number of Defined Prospects and Key Defined Prospects identified must be manageable. Too many firms target quantity, not quality. There is no point in generating a Defined Prospect base that cannot be pursued in any concerted way by nominated individuals and teams who have many other commitments.

Most of our marketing (which we examine in the next chapter) will be aimed toward Defined Prospects and Key Defined Prospects. However, we will need to adopt our most strategic and focused approaches to winning those most attractive Key Defined Prospects. This strategic approach is discussed overleaf.

Populating the Database

When creating its database a firm should also register all of the organisations that it has examined using its selection criteria including those that it has decided to classify as P0. Alongside the name of these entities should be a code or a note that explains why this organisation was not considered to be a desirable Defined Prospect. This code or note should also be dated.

This may seem like a lot of work to go through for an organisation that the firm has no interest in pursuing contact with. However this is a short term view. No doubt the firm will, within a few years, be re-examining the marketplace looking for new opportunities. Another practice area may repeat the exercise within months. So often we have seen businesses re-plough the same furrow because no one had kept any record of the prospects that had been consciously left (but not recorded as left) in the P0 zone outside of The PACE Pipeline.

A STRATEGIC APPROACH TO KEY DEFINED PROSPECTS – LANCHESTER STRATEGY

The Military Connection

In our workshops on business development we very often use a flipchart to draw a picture. The picture is of a lone soldier armed with a rifle. In front of him is a tall, rocky mountain and perched on top of the mountain is a fortified castle – a bit like the schloss in the old film, *Where Eagles Dare*. Minefields pepper the approaches to the edifice and the only track is exposed and covered by enemy guns. We explain to the workshop that this soldier is part of an army advancing into enemy territory and this particular fellow is faced with this terrain immediately to his fore. A general comes up from behind the soldier and says, "You've drawn lucky today. You have been presented with a target that any soldier in our army would be delighted to tackle. When you take this enemy stronghold your name will go down in history as a hero of our nation. Good luck, soldier." The general then disappears.

We turn to the workshop group and say, "OK. Put yourself in this guy's shoes. The general has disappeared. What would you do?" Nobody has ever suggested storming the castle single handedly. There are lots of jokes. "I'd dig a very deep hole and jump into it." "I'd work on a strategic plan, probably for a few months – then I'd review it. Hopefully the war would be over by then." "I'd shoot the idiot general." And so on. A lot of the comments border on the stupid – but then the initial scenario we presented had set the tone. It's somewhat like a marketing partner saying to one of his colleagues, "We've allocated our key prospects John, and you've been lucky enough to draw BP. I just know that you can get us in there and when you succeed your name will be associated with that client forever. Good luck John."

There have been many books written over the last few years that draw the parallels between what it takes to be successful in the military context and what it takes to be successful in the business world. Books like *Corporate Combat, Marketing Warfare* and *Sun Tzu and the Art of Business* use case studies of both military campaigns and business battles to make their points.

The real fundamental of military success has been known for centuries. Sun Tzu, a supremely successful Chinese General who lived more than two millennia ago and who wrote *The Art of War*, had the key. Napoleon Bonaparte knew the answer and once said, "God is on the side of the big battalions." A Prussian General, Carl von Clausewitz, in 1838 wrote a massive tome entitled *On War*. He penned the following. "Keep the forces concentrated in an overpowering mass. Always to be aimed at before all and as far as possible." This is known as the principle of force – and is the fundamental principle for military success. Success, Clausewitz was saying, is about concentration of one's forces. That is the very first thing that a general should be trying to achieve and he should be trying to achieve this aim to the greatest possible extent.

Again, Napoleon knew that success in battle came from having superior forces to the enemy "at the point that is to be attacked or defended." Here is the real key. Success is not about size. It is about the concentrated application of force at chosen points. This is why a mighty nation like the US could be humbled by a mainly guerrilla army in Vietnam. Some years after the Vietnamese war, a senior US General, looking back on the conflict said, "We forgot the lessons of Clausewitz."

It is why Napoleon in his 1796 Italian campaign with a force of 35,000 could defeat a combined Sardinian / Austrian army of 60,000. Knowing that the forces that faced him were in two separate camps with a weak point between them, Napoleon threw his entire army at the smaller Sardinian force, decimating them. He then turned his largely intact army against the Austrians, winning another great victory. Unfortunately at Waterloo, when Napoleon sent Marshall Ney off to sort out the Prussians before turning his attention to the British, Ney's execution was poor and the Prussians arrived with a significant force late in the day of the main battle. The rest, as they say, is history.

And history may have dealt more kindly with General Custer at the Battle of the Little Big Horn. If only the Indians had come over the hill one at a time he may have gone down as a hero. Unfortunately Crazy Horse's braves did not oblige and instead kept their force in an overpowering mass. The result was a massacre. Our flip chart with one lone soldier staring up at a heavily defended enemy stronghold is just an exaggerated example of the antithesis of a very simple principle.

Whilst virtually everyone will have heard of Napoleon, Rommel and Alexander the Great, our experience is that no one (virtually) has heard of Frederick Lanchester. Considering the man's achievements in his lifetime this is astounding. Lanchester, who was English, was born in 1868 and died in 1946. He was an engineer, a mathematician and a military strategist. He was a latter day Leonardo da Vinci. He built the first petrol driven four-wheeled motor vehicle in the UK in 1895. Amongst dozens of inventions he invented and patented disc brakes, rack and pinion steering, the pre-selector gearbox and automatic engine lubrication. He built the first armoured cars and many of the concepts that he introduced in his 1916 publication *Aircraft in Warfare* were used during World War Two. Lanchester Polytechnic kept his name alive for a number of years until it became Coventry University but the university's new library – built in 2000 – is named in his honour. For more about Frederick Lanchester visit the website www.lanchester.com.

During the First World War Lanchester turned his mind to military strategy. The battlefield had changed considerably in recent decades and the attentions of the so-called most civilised nations were directed at finding ever more fiendishly effective ways of killing their enemies. Concentration of force no longer meant having more troops than the enemy. The efficiency of the weapons used by both sides had a major impact on the likely outcome of a battle.

Lanchester arrived at two mathematical formulae – one that related to battle situations in 'traditional' warfare and one that related to modern warfare where the efficiency of the weaponry was highly significant. By using this second formula a modern military officer should be able to calculate the firepower and fighting men needed to take a military objective. Lanchester strategy was based on:

- Intelligence
- Concentration of firepower
- Dominance of positions taken.

Whilst Lanchester's formula may have been studiously overlooked by the British generals commanding forces on the Western Front, the Americans did take notice some time later. In the Pacific Theatre during the Second World War the US military used Lanchester's formula to calculate the forces required to take Japanese held islands. The US forces were steadily driving the Japanese back across the Pacific in their 'island hopping' campaign. Each and every island was taken but it was critical that the attacking forces were of sufficient concentration to enable the objective to be taken. At the same time resources (even for the US) were not limitless. Lanchester's calculation provided the basis for formulating a force with the requisite firepower.

The Commercial Application of Lanchester Strategy

After his death the name Lanchester all but disappeared from the public consciousness. However in the 1970s Lanchester's principles and formulae suddenly became interesting to the Japanese. Their interest this time was not in military application but in commercial application. The commercial application was all about:

- Intelligence of the market, customers and competitors
- Concentration of marketing and business development effort
- Dominance of customers and markets won.

Consultancies specialising in helping their clients to apply the principles of Lanchester Strategy sprang up. Marketing supremos belonged to Lanchester Societies. Major Japanese companies adopted Lanchester Strategy as their underpinning marketing principle. Honda came to dominate the world motorcycle market using Lanchester Strategy.

All this may seem far removed from marketing the services of a professional services firm. However, let us return to the picture of the soldier facing the fortress and the ridiculous notion that he could ever win through in such a situation. Let us also re-visit the almost equally ridiculous notion that a fee-earner be allocated a top FTSE 100 prospect and be expected to win this organisation as a client. Where's the concentration of force?

There is a perverse logic to the way that many firms go about pursuing new clients in their marketplace. If a person (or a practice area) has four Key Defined Prospects to pursue then by doubling this number to eight, one also doubles the chances of winning work from one of them. How much safer then to double this number – then double it again? With 32 Key Defined Prospects we are practically assured of having a win whereas with just four the risk of not winning any one of them seems high.

This 'safety in numbers' argument seems to make sense but in fact it is flawed. What happens when we have 32 points to attack is that we spread our forces – perhaps to the point of them being practically useless. We fly in the face of the principles of Clausewitz and Lanchester. The resources used for new business development in any firm are defined and limited. A firm must make the tough decisions about which small subsection of the prospect base that it is going to concentrate its forces upon. Even harder it has to decide which prospects it will not be actively pursuing. As Henri Bergson once said, "To choose means to exclude."

So how does a firm, practice area or market facing group implement Lanchester Strategy? The process has 11 stages.

Stage 1   Selection of targets
This has been the subject of the major part of this chapter.

Stage 2   Selection of 'task force'
One thing should already be very evident. Successful major new client acquisition is not achieved by allocating targets to individuals and then expecting them to go and hunt out the opportunities by themselves. This is a team game. It is by combining the knowledge and abilities of a number of people that we create the concentration of force needed to win a substantial new client. Teams do not need to be 20 strong. For Key Defined Prospects the team may have five or six members. On the other hand it may be just two or three people, but these individuals must be the most appropriate people for the job – not who is available.

Stage 3   Agreement to intelligence required about the Defined Prospect

We will already have some information about the Defined Prospect in question. The fact that we have chosen this organisation to target means, that by definition, we know something about them. However, if we are to mount a campaign that will really have effect, we probably need more intelligence. For instance, who are the key players in their organisation that we should be targeting? What exactly are these people responsible for? Which of our competitors are they using today – and for what type of work? What internal capabilities do they have and how sophisticated are they as clients?

Stage 4   'Satellite' observation

— meet/call key people go to

By this we mean gathering information usually available in the public domain. The prospective client's website is the starting point along with getting hold of all printed information such as corporate brochures and Report and Accounts. Again these may be available from the website. It may be useful to visit the websites of the Defined Prospect's main competitors to gain a comparative view. Almost certainly the prospect will be part of some industry association, so contacting them may prove helpful. News feeds, cuttings services and trade press may provide information. We may know of people who work for the prospect. Talking with them should be considered as well as talking with other (non-competing) advisors who have relationships.

Someone on the team must have overall responsibility for this intelligence gathering exercise. Whilst he or she will not carry out every element of the process, this person will be responsible for making sure that each person who is a part of this process carries out their role. This co-ordinator is responsible for pulling together all the data gathered.

Stage 5   Yes / No decision point

Too often this sort of initiative develops a momentum of its own. A team has decided to pursue prospect x and nothing will deflect them from this. Anything that is not an eventual client win must be, by definition, a defeat. However, there is a difference between a defeat and a tactical withdrawal and a team should meet and together they should:

- Share the intelligence gained. At some point the intelligence coordinator must decide that the team has got about as much data as it is likely to get from 'public' sources. The danger of 'analysis paralysis' has to be avoided.
- Make a decision (based on the information to hand) as to whether the prospect in question is still a suitable candidate for a Lanchester approach. It may not be – in which case the team should drop the prospect and consider other candidates that are more fitting for the application of Lanchester Strategy.

If the Key Defined Prospect is taken forward then the team should reconsider its composition. Based on what has been learned so far, does the team have the best mix of members to approach the prospective client?

Are some surplus to requirements – having knowledge and skills unlikely to assist in the pursuit of this prospect's business? Does the team need to recruit other members who are likely to bring more applicable abilities?

Stage 6   Creation of prospect's willingness to engage in dialogue

We know that at some point we have to engage directly with the prospective client. We have to meet with decision makers across their desks or in their conference rooms and talk business. The fact is that these people are busy and they already have advisors who, ostensibly, do the same things that we say we can do. Also, most likely, they have some loyalty to these advisors. After all, they appointed them. Added to which these advisors are probably doing a reasonably good job – this is a sizeable and prestigious client, which is why we are adopting a Lanchester approach. Why wouldn't the incumbents be concentrating on doing a really good job for this organisation that we are targeting?

If we are fortunate and there are people within the Defined Prospect that we know, then we should be setting up meetings with them. In fact we should probably have been doing this back in Stage 4. Very often, in the real world, there are no such lucky shortcuts. We don't conveniently know the CEO. The FD is not a member of our golf club. We are starting from scratch. These sorts of people need to be aware of our firm and to know what we can do. At some point we have to find ways of making them believe that we are very good at what we do – probably better than the people they are using today. Our marketing efforts have to achieve this and in Chapter 3 we will examine exactly what tools we have and how we should use them in order to get the people that we want to talk with, to want to talk with us.

Stage 7   On the ground 'spying'

The aim of our marketing effort is clear. We have to be invited through that Defined Prospect's door, into their reception area and then through into their meeting rooms.

All too often professionals have the wrong perspective on these early meetings with prospective clients. These meetings are seen by many as selling opportunities – and selling is about convincing the prospective client. It is obvious that to convince the other person that you have to pitch – putting forward cogent points and arguments. So one plans exactly what one wishes to convince the prospective client about and at the first opportunity launches into the pitch. *observe*

What can be forgotten is that the overall objective is to win the client. It is not to win the client today. In fact such a rushed approach will probably mean that the first meeting may well be the last. Early meetings are still a part of the intelligence gathering. They are the first opportunity to move from electronic intelligence to human intelligence (HUMINT as it is called in the spy books).

HUMINT is not gathered by talking. It is gathered by listening. In Chapter 4 we will look in some more detail how these meetings should be structured and some of the intelligence that a professional should be trying to gather.

NCOC -> No discussion yet

Stage 8   Yes / No decision point

Be Honest   Relegate

Just as we suggested at Stage 5, a Lanchester approach to a Key Defined Prospect should not be perpetuated by its own momentum. It should go forward because the team believes that the expenditure of energy and resources will bring commensurate wins and rewards. At some point after the early meetings with the Key Defined Prospect the team should reconsider the situation.

Face to face meetings with the prospective client can reinforce the team's hunger to win part of their work. On the other hand it is possible that we can learn things that make the prospect seem a lot less desirable. It may become clear that the way that they deal with professional advisors is very different to any relationship that we would want to engage in with a major client. We may find that the incumbents have cemented their relationship in ways that we would find difficult to emulate – and that may be against the ethics of the way we work. We may discover that their decision making process is complicated and fragmented and that work has to be won from a multiplicity of points making the relationship difficult to manage and any individual instruction expensive to win.

Decisions need to be taken. Do we continue to approach this Defined Prospect using Lanchester Strategy? Do we continue with the same team?

Stage 9   Concentrated attack

Egypt

If the decision is taken to continue, then the firm must then ensure that the resources are available in order to continue a prolonged penetration of the prospective client. The best prospective clients are nearly always another firm's key clients and it should be anticipated that they will be well defended and the siege may take a long time. It should be pointed out (in case there is misunderstanding) that we are not attacking the prospective client, but the competitors who are currently entrenched within that client. In Chapter 4 we will look at how we can continue this sort of campaign and some of the tactics that we can use.

Stage 10   Establish bridgehead and defend

At some point in a successful Lanchester approach we will win an initial piece of work. Our experience suggests that this initial instruction will not be large. That is a high risk decision for a client to make. To defend this initial bridgehead it is imperative that the fee-earning work is executed impeccably. The client's first impression of engaging the firm should be superb in terms of the way the work is planned, executed and managed and in respect of the way we communicate with the client during the lifetime of the project or instruction. On the basis of such excellent management of the fee-earning work we should be well placed to win similar instructions.

Stage 11   Seek to expand areas of work

One of the dangers of developing a great reputation with a client in a particular area of work is that we can become typecast. This is one of the barriers to cross-selling that we examine in Chapter 5, where we also examine what we can do to reduce this problem. We need to guard against this 'pigeon holing' as the firm probably has other areas of strength that it could equally deliver to the client.

Applying a Lanchester approach

So often when explaining the application of Lanchester strategy to clients someone will say, "This is not new. Do you know that's almost exactly how we won the business from XYZ. We may not have carried out every stage quite as rigorously as the model suggests and we didn't know it was called Lanchester Strategy but we were pretty much in line with the process." The problem with this observation typically is that after the success no one captured the essence of the approach and distilled it. Therefore the approach has probably rarely been replicated since – and if it has then only by accident. Lanchester Strategy is not new. The principle of force is not new. Neither is the law of gravity. They are all to do with physics – or the application of the principles of physics. The key is to recognise the principle and to harness it.

It is not uncommon for clients to say to us, "One of our main problems is focus, or rather a lack of consistent focus, in our business development activities." Concurrently however there is a pervading fear of 'too many eggs in one basket' and there is a real resistance to the implementation of a focused approach to business development. If we follow an unstructured approach to try to win a small number of potentially highly lucrative prospective clients then the eggs fear is a real concern. However, by rigorous implementation of Lanchester Strategy, using the opt out Yes / No points appropriately we have a process that can help win the most prestigious and lucrative new clients.

WHERE TO GO FROM HERE

Where to go from here if you run a firm or have overall responsibility for marketing and business development

Make it a rule that every part of the firm must have a set of P1 Defined Prospects and Key Defined Prospects and that these prospective clients must have been identified through the application of relevant filter and trigger selection criteria.

Champion, and take continued interest in, a couple of Lanchester approaches aimed at winning work from the firm's most attractive prospective clients.

Where to go from here if you run a business unit within a professional firm

Sit down with a group of people from your business unit and reach clear conclusions as to the type of client that you should be trying to build into your 'designer' client base of the future.

Then work out the specific selection criteria that will help you to identify the most attractive Defined Prospects from this market sector.

Assign someone to be responsible for carrying out the application of your chosen selection criteria – thereby leading to the identification of your business unit's P1 Defined Prospect base.

Choose one or two of your most attractive prospective clients and consciously adopt a Lanchester approach with the aim of opening them up as a new client of the firm.

Where to go from here if you are a marketing or business development professional working with fee-earners

Work with a receptive group in the firm that recognises that it needs to win new work from the marketplace and introduce them to the concept of filter and trigger selection criteria. Work with them to select the factors that will identify for them the most attractive Defined Prospects.

Take responsibility for managing the process of applying the chosen selection criteria to this group's prospective clients and help them to agree a final list of Defined Prospects and Key Defined Prospects.

Gain commitment from one of the groups that you work with to run a 'full blown' Lanchester approach directed toward a significant prospective client. Become a part of this team. You should be able to make significant contributions at most of the first nine stages in the application of Lanchester Strategy process.

Where to go from here if you are an individual practitioner within a professional firm

Draw up your own list of selection criteria that would typify those prospective clients that would be of most interest to you in the future.

Examine any prospects that you are currently pursuing (or intend to pursue). How well do these prospects match with your criteria?

Before becoming heavily involved in following up any future opportunities that may come your way, run any new prospects by your selection criteria to see how well they match up. Don't pursue those where there is a poor match.

Take one of the most significant prospective clients that you have been allocated or that you just have a yearning to win work from. Instead of approaching this as a solo effort see if you can encourage an appropriate team to form in order to approach the prospect using the application of Lanchester Strategy. Stick to the stages, one after the other.

Chapter 3   **Promoting**

THE EFFECT OF DIFFERENT PROMOTIONAL ACTIVITIES – AN EXERCISE

It is a curious paradox that whilst many professionals believe that they know very little about marketing and promotional tools, they in fact know a great deal. Why do we say that? An exercise that we have performed countless times on client workshops goes as follows. A flip chart sheet is prepared in advance. It appears as below.

What promotional tools / activities get prospective clients to:

Be aware of our
firm?

Know exactly
what we do?

Believe that we
can do it – and
better than
our competitors?

Take action and
give us work?

We then ask participants to think about any promotional tools and activities that they are aware of and to estimate how far down the sheet these activities typically take a prospective client. So, for instance, we have our advertising. Does our advertising typically get prospective clients to the point of wanting to utilise our capabilities? Probably not. Does the exposure convince prospective clients that we are definitely superior to our competitors? We may make claims that we are, but as far as convincing our Defined Prospects, then probably not again. However, our advertising should be able to raise awareness of our firm in the minds of prospective clients. Most advertising fits opposite the heading 'Be aware of our firm'.

Participants are asked for suggestions of activities and tools and to tell us where to place them down the right hand side of the flip chart. This type of session is typically quite lively with challenges flying left and right. Most challenges occur because the mental image that one person may have of (say) a seminar is very different to the image that is in the mind of one or more of his colleagues. We have learned over the years to qualify with the person putting forward the suggestion what exactly they mean. "Guest speaker" could mean being chosen to present to people from our own profession at a professional dinner. Very good for the ego to be selected before one's peers – but not always a powerful marketing tool. On the other hand it may mean addressing a client industry conference as a subject matter expert in a topic that is about to have a major impact upon the industry in question. The fact that the organisers have chosen us as the subject matter experts is an endorsement in itself. The delivery of a highly credible, useful and informative presentation will probably ensure that this type of marketing activity sits closer to "Believe that we can do it – and better that our competitors" than to "Know exactly what we do."

Most professionals want to get quickly to the factors that sit toward the bottom of the page. After all, that is where the new fee-earning work comes from. At some point someone will (rightly) suggest that "Take action and give us work" will typically only be achieved if there is a proposal submitted. And, if a proposal is needed, then probably there will need to be face to face meetings with the potential new client – and perhaps a presentation of some kind. Aren't we now talking more about selling rather than marketing? Indeed we are at this point.

The fact is that in nearly all instances we cannot promote our way to winning a new client. What our promotional activities can (and should) do is to pave the way for a successful selling opportunity to a very receptive prospective client. We do not want to open an academic debate on what marketing is and how this is different to business development. We use the flip chart exercise to illustrate (amongst other things) that there is a continuum of activities that lead toward the winning of new business and that marketing is not some activity divorced from, and separate to, business development.

In the development of new business we see the role of promotion, ultimately, to be very simple. **Our Promoting efforts should get the people that we want to talk with, to want to talk with us.**

So, how does this exercise typically conclude? An example appears on the next page.

Remember that this exercise has been conducted with professionals, many of whom say initially that they don't understand marketing and promotional tools. Many are sceptical of the value of marketing. Other than clarifying exactly what participants mean by their suggestions, our role in the workshop environment is to be secretarial, not editorial. We note down their submissions on the part of the flip chart that they (and their colleagues) have agreed. In fact most professionals, with a little thought, have a good understanding of promotional tools and their uses. Paradox answered.

THE EFFECT OF DIFFERENT PROMOTIONAL ACTIVITIES – CONCLUSIONS

One question that we always ask at the end of this exercise is, "What patterns do you see in your conclusions?" Not unexpectedly someone will suggest something along the lines of, "The things toward the top of the sheet are very broad, reach a wide audience and are 'broadcast' in nature. The things at the bottom are typically very specific, very often specific to one prospective client or even one person within that target organisation."

Once, when this question was asked of a group of technology consultants, one person replied, "The things at the top of the list are the most expensive – they cost more." The person sitting right next to her turned and said, "No, that is completely wrong. The items at the bottom of the list are the most expensive!" The first person to have commented was the Divisional Marketing Manager. The second to speak was the Divisional Director. What the Marketing Manager was saying is that in terms of pounds and pence the tools and activities at the top take far more of her budget. What her colleague meant was that the factors toward the bottom of the sheet take more consultant time and that has a high opportunity cost element, as every hour spent on marketing and business development activities is an hour that cannot be used for fee-earning. They were both correct.

A third conclusion that emanates from the exercise is that the promotional activities that really influence clients are nearly all carried out by the firm's professionals or, in some organisations, client-facing business development executives and account managers. Sure, marketing and support people can help in the setting up of some of these activities, but the enactment is usually down to professional staff.

What promotional tools / activities get prospective clients to:

Be aware of our firm?	Sponsorship	
	Corporate advertising	
	Mass corporate entertainment	
	Mailshots	
	General PR	
	'Ballroom scale' seminars	
	Articles in our own trade press	
	Entry for / winning of (our) industry awards	
Know exactly what we do?	Brochures	
	Websites	
	Directory entries	
	Newsletters	
	Publishing case studies	
	Conduct of proprietary research and / or client industry benchmarking studies	
	Publishing of research outputs	
	Subject matter expert (SME) articles in clients' trade press	
Believe that we can do it – and better than our competitors?	Speaking as subject matter expert (SME) at client industry conferences	
	Speaking at individual client conferences and meetings	
	Networking with prospective clients at conferences, events and meetings	
	'One-on-one' client / prospective client hospitality	
	Industry / issue–specific small scale workshops	
	Industry / issue-specific roundtable events	
	Referrals and references from existing clients	
	Issue-specific (SME) training for prospective clients	
	Surgeries	
Take action and give us work	Face-to-face 'selling' meetings	
	Proposals	
	Presentations / pitches	

So often we have come across marketers in professional firms who say to us, "We can't get our professionals to recognise the contribution that they have to make toward marketing the firm. They expect us to do it all and when new clients aren't knocking on the door they say things like, 'What are you doing with all that budget that we give you?'." Using the exercise above, we have never had any problem in getting professionals to see where their role lies in marketing for new work. They are clever people, this exercise is a simple one and the conclusions they draw are their own – and obvious.

We have sometimes observed radical shifts in belief after this 45 minute exercise. People who have started with the attitude of, "Why aren't we better known in our marketplace?", have been known to comment toward the end of the process, "Why do we bother with all of the stuff at the top – particularly as it costs so much? Why don't we concentrate our resources on the things that convince prospects that we are really good at what we do and therefore the sort of people that they should be talking to about new work?"

The answer to this is that a firm has to use marketing tools and activities to achieve different objectives. If the objective is to raise profile and brand awareness then the tools and activities at the top of the sheet will be most appropriate. If the objective is to take a group of prospective clients (who probably know us by name and have a reasonable idea of what it is that we do) to the point of convincing them to include us in their next Invitation to Tender (ITT), then a whole set of other activities are going to be more appropriate. The fact is that in any one period a firm probably has a number of marketing objectives and therefore will use a number of tools and activities concurrently.

However, the mistakes that many firms have made are:

- Too much of the promotional activity is delegated to the marketing department which leads, almost inevitably, to marketing being divorced from the fee-earners' activities and to a heavy focus on 'top of the sheet' promotional activities. In the worst cases, marketing departments measure their success by the size of the budget they are allocated each year.

- The professionals in the firm have false hopes that 'top of the sheet' promotional activities will lead to increased business development opportunities. This is wishful thinking.

Little wonder that some fee-earners have a low regard for marketing and see it mostly as an overhead.

NEARNESS TO CLIENT – CORPORATE, CAPABILITY AND CONTACT MARKETING

The output from the exercise examined above usually falls neatly into a model that we initially introduced in our first book, Creating New Clients. The model is known as the Nearness to Client Pyramid.

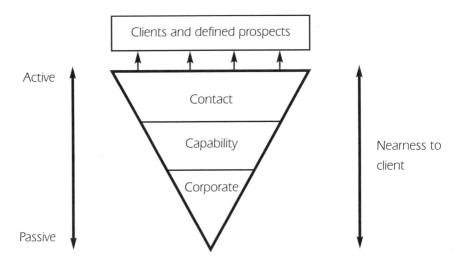

Corporate marketing activities are those activities that create a general awareness and understanding about what the firm does in general.

Capability marketing activities are those activities that specifically illustrate the firm's capabilities and what it can do for clients.

Contact marketing activities are those activities that involve direct contact between the prospective client and people from the firm. In addition, they seek to demonstrate the firm's understanding and support of its clients / prospects and to add value based on this understanding. It is these marketing activities that can differentiate a firm from its competitors.

If we take the earlier exercise and turn the answers upside down, then the model becomes populated with activities that fall into the different categories.

THE KEYS TO REALLY EFFECTIVE PROMOTIONAL EFFORTS

Rule One – Deliver Value

Let's not forget the simple aim of promotion directed toward our Defined Prospects. **We want the people that we want to talk with, to want to talk with us.**

What promotional tools / activities get prospective clients / to:

Be aware of our firm?	Sponsorship	Corporate marketing
	Corporate advertising	
	Mass corporate entertainment	
	Mailshots	
	General PR	
	'Ballroom scale' seminars	
	Articles in our own trade press	
	Entry for / winning of (our) industry awards	
Know exactly what we do?	Brochures	Capability marketing
	Websites	
	Directory entries	
	Newsletters	
	Publishing case studies	
	Conduct of proprietary research and / or client industry benchmarking studies	
	Publishing of research outputs	
	Subject matter expert (SME) articles in clients' trade press	
Believe that we can do it – and better than our competitors?	Speaking as subject matter expert (SME) at client industry conferences	Contact marketing
	Speaking at individual client conferences and meetings	
	Networking with prospective clients at conferences, events and meetings	
	'One-on-one' client / prospective client hospitality	
	Industry / issue–specific small scale workshops	
	Industry / issue-specific roundtable events	
	Referrals and references from existing clients	
	Issue-specific (SME) training for prospective clients	
	Surgeries	
Take action and give us work	Face-to-face 'selling' meetings	Business development / selling
	Proposals	
	Presentations / pitches	

So why would someone with whom we have never before talked business, ever want to talk with us? After all they will have existing advisors and it is not unreasonable to assume that those existing advisors will value the relationship with their client and therefore be carrying out high quality, well-regarded work. Additionally, engaging in dialogue with our firm will complicate life for our Defined Prospect. Instead of considering (say) three options on the next occasion they are seeking to appoint an advisor, they will now have to consider four.

There is one simple reason why a Defined Prospect will want to talk with us, irrespective of the relationship they have with their existing advisors. The reason is that on previous occasions, when the prospective client has come into contact with our firm, she has received some form of value from the contact. She may have read an article that was very relevant to her business, she may have heard one of our people speaking very authoritatively on a subject of interest to those in her industry or she may have attended a workshop that she found very helpful. Given this background of positive experiences the prospective client has every expectation that any further contact with our firm is likely to be equally useful and rewarding.

The marketing activities that have greatest impact on clients and prospective clients are those that deliver value to them. This point has been emphasised a number of times in an excellent programme of market research conducted by Nisus Consulting. Nisus has periodically examined the relationships between major clients and their legal advisors in the UK marketplace. The interviewers met with the Company Secretary or General Counsel of almost half of the FTSE 100 companies. Key clients by anyone's standards, these people had spent hundreds of millions of pounds on legal services in the previous 12 months. The interviews lasted between one hour and two and a half hours and the information gained was both quantitative and qualitative.

As far as marketing activities were concerned the ones that had greatest impact on these clients, and were welcomed most, were those where they obtained value for the time invested. The more educational and client-specific the activity, the greater the positive impact. There was a tepid response from these clients to newsletters. The more generic the newsletter, typically the more tepid the response. Some thought that lunches could be valuable – but only if they contained a business / knowledge sharing / information giving element. The responses to corporate entertainment varied but in general contributors did not feel it affected the way they awarded future work. Some, however, were disparaging with one respondent quoted as saying "Throwing away our money on entertainment makes us mad."

Therefore we should look at our promotional activities through our Defined Prospect's eyes and consider what value we are delivering through that activity.

Rule Two – Create the opportunity to judge what it is like to work with us

How many times have professionals told us that theirs is a people business – that people do business with people, that people buy from people?

We need no convincing. We are in violent agreement!

However let us qualify this just a little. People do business with people they know. People buy professional services from people that they trust.

Therefore our promotional activities should not only be seeking to deliver value to our Defined Prospects. They should also, ideally, be providing these prospective clients with the opportunity to get to know and trust us – to allow them to make early judgements about our credibility, competence and compatibility with them and their business.

PROMOTIONAL ACTIVITIES AND TOOLS IN THE LIGHT OF THE TWO RULES

Corporate Marketing Activities

Sometimes our conclusions on Corporate Marketing are misconstrued. We are seen to be 'anti' Corporate Marketing activities. We are not. We see very little value however, on a heavy emphasis on the use of Corporate Marketing tools with a corresponding and concurrent low focus on Contact Marketing activity.

Corporate advertising

Corporate advertising, whether in the press, on television, on posters or in any other medium, puts the firm's name in front of hundreds of clients, thousands of potential clients and millions of people who have absolutely no interest in ever working with us. Done well, it is proven to work. What we mean by this is that a well-constructed advertising campaign can increase name awareness. Firms that are serious about increasing awareness of their business should allocate something like 20% of their advertising budget to measuring name awareness before and after the campaign. Most don't, they prefer to buy additional space with the money – then carp later that they can't measure the effectiveness of their marketing!

Despite increasing awareness in the marketplace, advertising in isolation delivers absolutely no value to potential clients and gives the prospect no real idea of what it is like to deal with us. Corporate advertising works well when it is part of a wider campaign or message – which sees the firm investing in all three levels of the pyramid. It generates more value for money when used in this integrated approach.

Corporate entertainment

When conducting the workshop exercise outlined at the beginning of this chapter, the time when the debate really starts to buzz is when someone suggests, "Corporate hospitality" or "Corporate entertainment." This is one of those occasions when we have learned to ask, "What exactly do you have in mind?"

Firstly, it is our experience that the vast majority of corporate hospitality results in being a "thank you", not a "please." In other words, it is attended to a very large extent (and sometimes exclusively) by clients, rather than prospective clients.

Secondly, it is often the 'usual suspects' who turn up to the free outing and for the free food and drink.

Thirdly, the event too often reflects the interests of the senior professionals in the firm rather than the clients who are invited.

Finally, for many of these events there is a high late cancellation rate from invitees as they find more important things that they need to attend to closer to the date. This results in last minute invitations to 'lower grade' invitees and the filling of spare places by professionals who have nothing better to do on the day in question. They then claim the hours as 'marketing' or 'business development' on their time sheets.

If these are genuinely the results that a firm seeks to achieve from its expenditure on corporate entertainment then it is not for us to tell them they are wrong. It's their money.

Where the real debate usually focuses is in the difference between 'mass' corporate entertainment and small scale or 'one-on-one' client / prospective client hospitality. Let us take two examples.

Not long ago one of the major accounting firms used the Royal Ascot race meeting as one of its corporate hospitality events. Over the course of the week they put on coaches each day to transport their guests en masse to the racecourse 30 miles from London. Over the week some 400 guests were entertained. All-inclusive tickets worked out at about £400 a head. The firm had a marquee and provided all food and drink for its invited guests. You guessed it. Nearly all the people who turned up were clients, mostly the 'usual suspects' who appreciated a 'freebie' and the people who dropped out at the last moment were the more senior client contacts who found pressing business issues that overrode the 'nice to have' day at the races. One wonders, given the lavishness of the entertainment provided, if those who attended could remember which racecourse they had been to, let alone who had invited them. A racecourse is also a huge area in which to roam and a race crowd is a very easy place to lose contact with one's hosts.

The second example is diametrically opposite. In this instance the property professional concerned had been talking with a prospective client for a number of months. Two senior managers had attended a workshop run by the firm, the professional had followed this up and he had met with the client on their premises. No specific opportunities had arisen from this meeting but the professional kept in contact and ensured that the prospective client received relevant mailings. During a second meeting some months later a chance remark revealed that the client was a keen golfer. The professional was also a golfer – of somewhat moderate ability – but his firm had corporate membership at a rather exclusive golf course. Would the client and a colleague like to join him for a round of golf? The professional was sure that he would be able to arrange for someone else to make up a foursome.

The client accepted the invitation in principle and during the next couple of weeks the details were agreed. Making up the foursome was a rather high profile client with whom the professional had a long-standing and very sound relationship.

Golfers (and at least one of the authors of this piece is not one) always jump at this story and tell us what a great opportunity it is to really get to know and understand someone over a game of golf that lasts three or four hours. You get to see the real person we are told. We accept this totally but the golfers must also accept that this is a two-way process. The prospective client is also forming a view of his host. Is this a person with whom I could have a close advisor relationship? Is his way of acting and behaving compatible with me and the type of people he would be working with in my company? Is he scrupulously honest? Is he assertive but not over-assertive? Does he listen or does he like the sound of his own voice? Is he sensitive to others' needs?

Small scale or one-on-one prospective client hospitality, if well conceived and executed, does allow the prospect to begin to form an opinion of what it might be like to work with us. In the case of the professional and his golfing foursome the prospective client's people were not only able to form an opinion of the professional, they formed an opinion of how he understood and worked with his existing clients. Moreover, the existing client was a subtle reference source for the prospective client's people. The answers that he provided to their questions gave them more evidence on which to base their judgement.

Immediately after the golfing day the professional sent a 'courtesy note' to his prospective clients saying that he had enjoyed their company and hoped that they had also found the day enjoyable. He followed up with a phone call a few days later at which time they told him that they were in the early stages of considering a transaction and would he like to come in and discuss the details? Several meetings, one proposal and one formal presentation later the professional and his firm won their very first piece of work from their prospective client.

Articles in our own trade press and entry for / winning of our industry awards

A client of ours once labeled these promotional activities as 'corporate self-gratification'. At issue here is who will see, and be influenced or impressed by, our article or award. If a lawyer writes an extremely clever article that appears in a publication read only by other lawyers in private practice, then he may receive the acclamation of his peers – if he is lucky. Most likely he will provide some free advice and education to his competitors whose thinking was not so well formed or leading edge. It is extremely unlikely that any of his firm's Defined Prospects will ever get to share these leading edge insights.

Similarly much time and effort can be expended in competing for industry awards. Even if a firm is successful in winning an award, do its Defined Prospects know? If the 'industry' means the firm's direct competitors – in the case of The PACE Partnership this would mean other business development consultancies – there is very little or no value in this exercise. If, however, the 'industry' includes at least as many clients, in-house experts and potential connections as competitors, then both the award and the exposure can help to raise name awareness. The most powerful recognition is achieved when the client industry votes a firm or a professional as being at the top of their profession. Seen to be the best franchising lawyer by the franchising industry is an accolade worth having.

Great care should be taken before investing in these promotional activities. In our experience too few have any real impact on our clients and even less on our Defined Prospects. Also as promotional tools they do not deliver any value to our Defined Prospects and they provide little evidence of what it is like to work with us.

Sponsorship

Sponsorship often suffers from one of the problems associated with corporate hospitality. The sponsorship can reflect the interests of the people at the helm of the firm rather than the likely interests of the firm's clients or Defined Prospects. No single sponsorship will fit well with all clients and prospective clients, that is obvious. However, some of the obscure causes and events that have been supported by professional firms from time to time would cause most of us to raise an eyebrow and question the motivation behind the decision.

The best sponsorship packages give a firm the opportunity to invite (interested) clients and prospective clients to the event (say a ballet) and to spend time with them. Again our experience is that these invitations are heavily focused toward current clients as a "thank you" and are not really a part of the effort of marketing for new work or new clients.

Also one should be realistic in what can be achieved at some events. A partner in one of the Big 4 accountancy firms told us of his experience of inviting a client and his wife to see the performance of an opera company that the firm was involved in sponsoring. He knew that the client and his partner were opera fans even though it was nothing more than a passing interest to him and his wife. However, he figured that he was directing his energy toward something that was of interest to the client (right) and that the evening gave him a good three hours or more with the client (wrong!). He told us – laughing at his own expense – that he realised just before the opera began that the 'quality' time with his client was restricted to the 30 minute interval, jammed in an overcrowded bar. Not much of a marketing activity but apparently the client and his wife enjoyed the performance.

('Ballroom Scale') seminars

In our Effect of Different Promotional Activities exercise that we carry out with professionals who participate in our workshops, one of the tools that is always mentioned is seminars. Again our response is, "Tell us what these seminars look like." At one end of the spectrum we have what some have termed the 'ballroom scale' seminars. These are typified by:

- Invitations that are sent out to all and sundry – very often in their hundreds if not thousands.

- A huge disparity in the 'quality' of the audience.

- A large number of late cancellations or people just not bothering to turn up.

- Last minute substitutions with junior people sent in place of their more senior colleagues who were originally invited – thereby reducing the quality of the overall audience.

- An overwhelming number of participants compared to the number of people from our firm who are also in attendance.

- Very little opportunity to speak to the people who have turned up for the seminar either before, or at the completion of, the event due to the 'tide of humanity' effect as people arrive and leave over a short period of time.

- A one-way broadcast message to the participants as it is impossible to engage a large audience in any form of meaningful dialogue or interplay.

A few year's ago a senior partner in one of the large accountancy practices told us that his firm's Budget Breakfasts were exactly like this and that he believed that they were an expensive waste of time from a marketing perspective. Budget Breakfasts were delivered the day after the UK's Chancellor of the Exchequer had told Parliament what would be in his next budget. During the late afternoon and all through the night the accountancy firms dissected the Chancellor's information, produced summary notes and reports that they had printed at huge expense and prepared a presentation that was delivered at breakfast the following morning. Invited clients (or their substitutes) arrived to have a free breakfast and to hear what the accountants had to say about the effect of the budget on their businesses. The exercise burnt time and money – and the candle at both ends for those managing and carrying out the analysis.

A manager who had participated in the firm's previous Budget Breakfast exercise in London (and who clearly thought that he had contributed to a very worthwhile event) turned to the Senior Partner and asked, "So why do we do them then?"

"We have to of course," replied the Senior Partner, "Because our competitors do them. We couldn't be seen to be the only major firm not running a Budget Breakfast!"

We are not critical of this partner's attitude. Rather the opposite. At least he was very clear in his mind what these types of events could (and couldn't) deliver as a marketing activity. He was under no illusion as to why he continued to support their existence at that time. (Fortunately, and partly due to a change in the timing of the Chancellor's speech, it is clear to us that this particular example of a ballroom seminar is much rarer now.)

Ballroom scale seminars fail the two tests for effective marketing activity. The bigger and more disparate our audience then the less likely we are to be able to deliver value to each of the individuals in the audience. Also any Defined Prospect who attends one of these events is provided with very little evidence of what it is like to work with us, day to day.

Capability Marketing Activities

Brochures

A few years ago David Maister, on the subject of brochures wrote, "The glossy equivalent of a business card. You need to have one but it won't do much for you."

Despite Maister's conclusion (which we endorse wholeheartedly) is that professionals within firms, in the main, still cling to the belief that they need brochures. They are like a security blanket. They appear to be solid, tangible, good quality collateral material that reflects the stature and nature of the firm's business. They can be sent to a Defined Prospect or can be left with a prospective client (sometimes in some vain hope that the donation of a brochure will undo a poorly conducted and unproductive early meeting with a prospect).

Yet when questioned on the subject we find that these same professionals admit to almost never reading brochures either sent to them or given to them by salespeople. Why then should a prospective client take the time to read our brochure?

Most of the corporate brochures we see we believe to be a waste of time and money. They tend to paint a very generic picture of the firm using glowing words and phrases ("client-focused", "in partnership with your management team", "commercially orientated" etc etc) that clients have heard and seen a hundred times before but have experienced almost never. They cut no ice with any discerning prospective client. Many of these firms should consider cutting the expense and investing the money that has been saved into (for example) improving – and regularly updating – their website. Or they could divert the investment in brochures into creating very tailored and well-produced proposals for Defined Prospects, which explain why they would like to work with them and the specific benefits that client would gain as a result.

Service-specific brochures or flyers can have some value. Case studies even more so. However it is questionable if they always need to be in printed format. In the electronic age it is not difficult to generate brochures that can be downloaded (perhaps in PDF format) from the firm's website. In that way, if a Defined Prospect is really interested in one of our capabilities or services, she can print off the relevant material or we can send it to her via e-mail. Again, if we genuinely have reason to believe that one of our capabilities is of particular interest, we can print off the relevant material in colour on good quality paper – perhaps with amendments tailoring the messages specifically to the prospect in question.

Websites

Professional services firms run the risk of their websites matching David Maister's views on brochures – that like business cards everyone expects you to have one but it won't do much for you. In our experience (and we have regular need to visit firms' websites) one site is very much like the next. The graphics may vary of course but the information that one consulting engineering firm (for example) provides is much the same as the rest of the firms in that marketplace.

Let us not forget the aim of marketing activities directed toward our Defined Prospects. **We are trying to get the people that we want to talk with, to want to talk with us.** To do this we have to be seen to deliver value in any contact that the Defined Prospect has with our firm and we must try to allow the prospective client to experience what it is like to work with us. Most websites don't begin to address these issues. They are electronic brochures – and, in the worst cases, out of date electronic brochures.

How can we deliver value? The answer is to provide information that prospective clients will find valuable. Articles and papers on client related subjects should be available on the site – either for people to read, interact with or easily download. This information or 'knowledge bank' should be updated and supplemented on a regular basis in order that any prospective client who returns to the site will find new information that is of value. The objective here is to provide value in any and every contact that the prospect has with our firm.

The more progressive firms are realising this, and offer added value materials such as industry reports, 'how to' guides, 'toolkits' and business trend monitors on issues relating to their clients' worlds. Those that invest in building sophisticated search technology into their site, also help clients find, very quickly, the information and help they are seeking.

If a prospective client is visiting two firms' websites and one gives useful information and insights readily whilst one is totally firm-centric, we should not be surprised that the prospect begins to draw conclusions as to what it is like to deal with each of these firms.

Newsletters

Every month we receive an electronic newsletter from an HR consultancy called HR Advantage. This is a small professional services firm with approximately six fee-earners. The format is simple and the bulletin is normally about four pages in length. Being partners in a firm and having some responsibility for employing others we find it useful to keep abreast of what is happening in the HR world – particularly in relation to new HR law.

The electronic format suits us as well. When we recognise the e-mail to which the newsletter is attached we immediately dump the attachment onto our desktops and read it at a convenient point during the next week or two. We are clearly not alone in our preference as in the Nisus Consulting research many of the clients who were interviewed said that they would prefer to receive newsletters electronically rather than in hard copy format.

What impressions are we usually left with, having read this newsletter? They are as follows:
- We've usually learned something – and usually in the space of ten minutes.
- These people have good attention to detail (no typographical errors or other mistakes).
- These people know a lot more about these subjects if we need to find out more.
- Across the small number of consultants in their firm they have a surprisingly wide range of, what appear to be, credible capabilities.
- The firm runs regular training courses that we could attend if we wish to gain further input in a number of areas.

On the last point, HR Advantage and other firms that produce newsletters for clients and Defined Prospects have to be careful. There is a danger that the newsletter becomes a 'push' tool and not a 'pull' tool. By that we mean that they may use them as a way to promote the firm and its chargeable services rather than to deliver value to their readers. When this happens readers will immediately cease reading. The newsletter becomes another piece of spam. The effectiveness of the tool disappears.

We think that the HR Advantage example is a good one. It demonstrates two things. Firstly, even very small firms that are really resource constrained can produce a regular newsletter. Secondly, the more focused the newsletter is on the issues the recipient is facing, the more valuable it will be.

However, we are now moving rapidly into those marketing activities that are primarily the remit of fee-earners. Experts need to have (at least) some input into 'mini articles' that make up a newsletter.

Articles in clients' trade press
We believe that there is great value in becoming a regular contributor of articles and material to the publications that are read by clients and Defined Prospects. This is where firms or practice areas that have a market sector focus have an advantage. They can readily identify the journals that are read by their target audience. In our experience trade journals are looking for good copy – articles relevant to their audience and expert comment from specialists who understand their readers' businesses.

Marketing support people can manage the conduit between the professional and the publication's editor or journalists – discussing the types of input that would be of interest and the timing of these. However, they cannot necessarily write the articles on their own. Article writing requires the commitment of fee-earners – either in:

- Providing detailed content for the article to a ghost writer (e.g. a marketing professional or PR consultant) and then proofing or editing it; or
- Relaying content directly to the trade title journalist; or
- Writing the article themselves

Fee-earners are not normally natural authors. On top of that they are usually asked to write about something that draws on their technical expertise. Making a technical topic accessible in a client trade magazine article is a challenge to even the most gifted of writers. So when sitting down to write an article the main motivation should be, "How do I give some form of value to the typical reader of this piece?"

In fact we would suggest that if the task is approached with any other motivation the article is unlikely to see the light of day. Editors readily spot the difference between a genuine article that will enhance the quality and standing of their publication in the eyes of their readers from 1200 words of self-promotion. Any attempt to self promote may mean that we are not asked to contribute in the future. Similarly, anything that uses a lot of technical language and unnecessary jargon will also be discarded by the trade journal.

Again, marketing or PR professionals provide great help here and can guide a fee-earner on the 'readability' of the piece. Together they and the fee-earner can make a piece that is both interesting in content and style and which grabs and holds the attention of the reader. They can also ensure it helps to build the positioning the firm wants for a particular issue or market.

Our own experience of using this marketing tool may provide useful input. We are regular contributors to some of the most widely read professional services publications in the UK. Our articles appear usually in the management section of the journal concerned. We have found that not only do we get name recognition ("Be aware of our firm") from this type of activity, but that we are recognised as being experts in our particular fields of focus ("Know exactly what we do"). The fact that a leading industry journal chooses to publish our thoughts is, in itself, something of an endorsement. From time to time, depending on the nature of the article, we receive direct contact from prospective clients who want to talk further with us about the subject on which we have written. Sometimes this is a bonus but one has to accept that not all the businesses that make direct contact with our firm are on our list of Defined Prospects.

Another bonus is that journalists, when working on other articles themselves, will sometimes call our offices and ask for thoughts on a subject or for a quote. In that way we also get our name in front of our clients and Defined Prospects – seen as offering 'expert comment'.

Building relationships with key journalists in their clients' trade press, enables a firm to take a more strategic approach to their PR efforts. Not only does this help to ensure they are the first port of call when the journalist has an issue they require a viewpoint on, they can start to feed the journalist with ideas for news or features pieces. The more insight we have of our clients' businesses and industries, the more we can identify articles or stories which we can pitch to their trade press (preferably for us to write or add expert comment to). This will ensure our firm's name soon becomes associated with real expertise on these issues.

That doesn't mean we should abuse our position of trust with our clients and Defined Prospects and expose them to unwanted media attention. Instead we should try and give general commentary, responding to trends and developments in a specific industry and offering practical help and insight into (for example) a piece of legislation which will impact on readers of that article.

So, identify the key journalists your firm wants to get close to. Treat them as you would your clients and Defined Prospects and build a position of competence, compatibility and credibility in their mind. Finally, manage the relationship so that if one journalist moves on (and they do fairly frequently from our experience), you still know plenty more and can maintain the same level of support and co-operation with that particular title.

Proprietary research and benchmarking studies

Research and benchmarking can be very effective promotional tools. For example, if you were the Chairman of a UK professional football team and you wanted to appoint a firm of financial advisors, who would be on your short list? We would suggest that two definite inclusions would be Deloitte and PKF. The reason for this is that as a football club Chairman you would be fairly certain that both really understood the industry issues with which you were dealing and they would probably already have some feel for the particular issues faced by your club.

One major reason that these two firms have such a deep understanding is that they carry out regular research into the football industry. The information that they gain allows them to understand the industry's emerging issues and to benchmark the relative positions of the clubs on which they have gathered data. Not unsurprisingly, both dominate as financial advisors to major clubs and act on a large number of football club restructuring programmes.

The Deloitte and PKF football example once again raises the issue of market focus. As a Financial Director I may be mildly interested in understanding the latest statistics on employee fraud in the country but as a Financial Director of a retail business I would probably be extremely interested to know where my business stood in relation to detected employee fraud in the retail sector. That delivers additional value and is more likely to motivate me to take the time and effort to participate in the initial data gathering stage.

Proprietary research does require input from senior professionals within a firm. The whole exercise cannot be passed to an outside research agency then just forgotten about until, some weeks later, some magical output appears. Professionals have to decide:

- What do we want to find out about?
- What will give us a better insight into our clients and prospective clients?
- What information would our clients and prospective clients find useful to their organisations and their specific job roles? (What would deliver value?)
- Who would be the people who would be likely to have this information?
- If the research is to draw on perceptions – what would be the most likely way to motivate individuals to share their opinions and information with the people who would be conducting the research?
- What format of output or reporting would be most useful for both people within our own firm and also for clients and prospective clients – some of whom may have participated in the research process and some who will not?
- How do we want to use the outputs?

Once the firm is clear on the answers to these questions then it is time to deploy more marketing resource and perhaps professional external agencies.

Fundamentally there are three different ways that proprietary research and benchmarking exercises can be carried out.

- The first is to pass the exercise to an external professional organisation that has a successful track record in conducting such research projects.
- The second is to involve an external professional organisation but to keep part of the work internally – especially if your people are going to have the edge and expertise to interpret the results.
- The third is to do-it-yourself – again if your firm holds the best people (in terms of their expertise and knowledge) to conduct the research and analyse the results.

In our experience all three approaches can be used successfully. It is a case of selecting the approach that best suits the research that is being proposed. In professional services, this tends to focus on three methods:

- Opinion-led studies – either by asking for people's views through questionnaires, interviews, focus groups or a combination of the three
- Data-led studies – for example analysis of performance statistics, financial and other such business data in the public domain
- A combination of the two – using opinion led studies to draw out the reasons for a particular statistic or piece of data, for example as part of a benchmarking exercise.

In our own business we have conducted several opinion-led benchmarking exercises as part of our marketing activities. We have benchmarked firms' practices in relation to new business development and also their key client management capabilities. The simple questionnaire took 20 to 25 minutes to complete and could be done in either hard copy or electronically on our website.

Every participant received a report on how well (in their opinion) their firm performed in each of twelve core aspects of key client management (ten core aspects in the case of new business development). At the conclusion of the research, after analysis of the data had been carried out, each participant was sent a benchmarking report. They could compare their (say) law firm with probably 25 peer businesses and a total of around 80 or 90 professional firms in total. In addition to the statistics we also provided commentary on each of the sectors and how they performed. Firms that did not participate in the research had the opportunity of purchasing the general benchmarking report after it had been sent to the participants.

Putting aside the benefits that our clients received from this information, this exercise was also an extremely useful plank in our marketing directed toward Defined Prospects. Why was that so?

Firstly, our knowledge of our chosen market improved.

Secondly, the research outputs provided extremely good core material for articles that were of interest to the professional services press. This was another way of reaching our target market.

Thirdly, the wider media took an interest in some parts of the report conclusions and published extracts. Appearing in the Financial Times was very motivating but we did not kid ourselves. This was Corporate Marketing, very much in the mould of "Be aware of our firm."

Fourthly, the insights that we gained into issues most affecting the various sections of the professional services marketplace enabled us to identify workshop and round table opportunities – another way of gaining audience with our Defined Prospects. We were also able to develop and improve our products and services.

Finally, many Defined Prospects who participated in the benchmarking exercise were very willing to meet to discuss their outputs and the issues that the report had drawn to their attention.

The latter two benefits were important. Good proprietary research and benchmarking (when used as a promotional tool) should always deliver value to participants – one of the two keys to really effective marketing. However, it can also unlock the opportunity to speak with Defined Prospects, providing them the with chance to form an opinion of what it is like to deal with us on a day-to-day basis – the second key.

One caveat on research. At the time of writing we notice more and more research being carried out as more and more firms recognise the potential benefits outlined above. The challenge now is to stand out to potential respondents, readers and editors alike, from the herd. High quality research carried out professionally, presented creatively and, most importantly, delivering insights of value to the audience remains a very effective tool; sub-standard research carried out 'because it seemed like a good marketing tool' is likely to sink without trace or, more worryingly, undermine rather than improve the firm's reputation. We should also be careful about how we interpret the research – especially if it is built on opinion and self-perception studies. People will have different motivations in how they respond to our questions and we may need to try and factor these in when we analyse the results to present a balanced view.

Conference speaking

Industry events

Conference speaking at client industry events is the verbal equivalent of writing articles in clients' trade press. As well as achieving most things that article writing can provide – such as giving the opportunity to deliver value to those in the audience – conference speaking delivers other benefits as a marketing activity.

- It provides the opportunity to target the audience for our messages more accurately.
- It gives prospective clients a chance to form an early opinion about what sort of people we are and what it might be like to work with us.
- The conference may provide other opportunities to make contact with prospective clients. This could be through networking during the breaks, offering to send electronic copies of slides to those who provide their business cards or by running a simple piece of research that attendees can easily engage in.

However, just as with article writing, effort has to be invested up front to identify those organisations, and the people in them, who run the types of conferences that we would be most interested in addressing. We have to be certain that their events are well organised with good quality participants attending. If not, then this activity can be a waste of time – and may even reflect badly on the speaker. Similarly, as with articles, if a professional uses the conference opportunity to explicitly promote his firm at the expense of delivering value in his messages, then he is unlikely to be invited a second time.

And, just like article writing, there are some people who are very good at this activity and some people who struggle. A firm should only allow the very best of its presenters to address key industry and client conferences. The decision should be made based primarily on communication skills. Technicians with poor communication skills or people with high egos but low projection, damage our marketing efforts and affect the audience's perception of our firm's image. The first message that they send out to prospective clients is, "These people aren't very professional or interesting." These are not the judgements that we want Defined Prospects to make in respect of what it may be like to work with us.

Where possible, we should try and build in a follow-up to any conferences we are asked to speak at. This could take the form of sending delegates a summary of the points we made, a copy of a relevant article / piece our firm has created on the subject, an invitation to participate in a piece of research on the issue discussed or drawing them to relevant hints / tips on our website. Whatever our correspondence, this follow-up should always add value to the recipient, and not plug our firm's services.

By conducting this follow up, we will remind the conference delegates of the content of our presentation and continue to reinforce our firm's credibility and competence in this field. We can also use it to build a more targeted communication that may encourage them to want to talk to us more about the issue covered in the conference.

Client events

Most conference speaking that professionals carry out is at industry events. However, there are occasions when professionals are invited by clients to address their own internal conferences and meetings. Whether the professional chooses to bill for this time depends on a whole raft of different factors. Whether billed or not, participating in these events is usually a good investment of time. Internal conferences almost always focus on the issues most close to the client's business. It's a great way of learning very quickly what the organisation is trying to achieve in the future and what the challenges are that the business faces. It is also an extremely good time to widen the number of client contacts that one has. Needless to say, the address to the audience is another medium by which the professional can demonstrate his value as an advisor to the business

Defined Prospect events

Now, instead of thinking 'client conference', think 'Defined Prospect conference'. Forget the decision about billing for the time. This is a marketing investment. The biggest decision made in this instance is not the professional deciding to forego a day's fee earning but the prospective client's decision to risk inviting an 'unknown quantity' to address an important company event.

We would suggest that if the timing is appropriate and the Defined Prospect has had some opportunity to become comfortable with us as potential advisors, then offering to participate in an internal corporate conference as a guest speaker could be a powerful marketing activity. Value can be delivered and we can create the opportunity to meet with people and for them to begin to form judgements about what we are like to work with.

Contact Marketing Activities

Networking

The two keys to effective marketing aimed at Defined Prospects are delivering value and providing the prospective client with the opportunity to judge what it would be like to work with us. As a specialist guest speaker at a client industry conference it would be possible to be wheeled in to make a presentation then wheeled back out again. Assuming that the address was well targeted then the first of our objectives would have been met. We have delivered value. The second though will hardly have been met at all.

We will have projected a public persona from a distance but not allowed prospective clients to form a true view of what kind of people we are. To achieve this we need to communicate with people on a one-to-one basis. Conferences, events and meetings are not only excellent platforms to show what great capabilities we have, they are also great opportunities for professionals to network with clients and prospective clients.

Many professionals shy away from this activity. It is something that they are not comfortable with and therefore the potential return on the (sometimes substantial) investment in attending and participating in an event is not fully realised. A lack of skill in being able to network semi-socially means that most attempts are uncomfortable and don't work well for the professional. This undermines confidence and leads to future avoidance of the activity. The key, therefore, is to address the behaviour – the skills. That is where the negative circle must be broken and where appropriate training is key.

It is clear that good networkers – people with the skills to communicate one-to-one in a mixed business / social environment – have a tremendous advantage. Prospective clients are forming opinions about them (probably mostly favourable) and gaining some perspective of what it may be like to work with the professional in question. The professional who has delivered his presentation and then gone back to his office has not properly entered the race for new clients.

Small scale workshops and round tables

We should begin by defining what we mean by a workshop and how this differs from a round table. In a workshop most of the input will be from the firm's presenters who will be subject matter experts (SMEs). Whilst participants may become engaged in some activities such as examining case studies and may ask questions to clarify points or (sometimes) to challenge the speakers, most of the flow of information – hopefully valuable – passes from speaker to audience.

At a round table session participants are expected to make a more significant contribution. A round table may begin with an SME outlining the issues and the ground to be addressed in the discussion but then he sits down and is involved no more or less than the other people who have been invited. These people are generally a mix of clients, prospective clients and others with specialist knowledge of the topic. A round table session also works best when an experienced facilitator chairs the discussion and maintains general direction and control.

Whether a round table or a workshop, some guidelines that apply are:

- Focus the session on an opportunity or business issue that is of current or future burning interest to a section of the firm's clients and prospective clients.
- Target the audience very carefully. The aim is not to have lots of people at these events. The aim is to have the right sort of people. The participation of too many 'low quality' attendees will drive the 'high quality' participants away from future workshops and round tables that the firm organises. Also be sensitive to any issues that might arise from inviting competitors to such events.
- Keep the numbers small – no more than 20 or so for a workshop and no more than 10 for a round table.
- Make sure that plenty of the firm's professionals are on hand for the event. This means the people who best understand the subject and the target audience – not those people whom it is discovered the day prior have nothing better to do. (A rough guide is one firm person to every four participants.)
- Ensure that the participants gain value from their attendance. In a workshop this is more within the firm's control because the firm's professionals largely determine the input. Despite the lack of control that the structure of a round table seems to engender, very often participants gain enormous benefit from such an event. Instead of listening to one or two subject matter experts they share real life experiences with their peers who are dealing with similar issues to themselves. When the insights of an SME need to be drawn upon the person is on hand.

The temptation is to direct these events solely toward the existing client base. Whilst they are useful marketing and relationship building activities for this audience they are tremendous marketing tools for the acquisition of new business relationships. For these types of events, the delivery of value should be a given.

However, workshops and round tables should also provide ample opportunity for prospective clients to enter into dialogue with the firm's people. This can happen before the event begins, at breaks and at the conclusion as well as during the sessions themselves. This is why it is important that the firm fields the right people not only in the SME role but also as 'hosts' for the event. The aim, once again, is to provide Defined Prospects with the opportunity to judge what it may be like to work with us.

A few other tips to ensure the best output from seminars and round tables are as follows:

- Make every effort to ensure that all invitations to in-house events are targeted toward the right audience. Address the invitation to the individual and address it correctly. With people who are well-known clients, find some way to personalise the invitation. Mass mailshots cheapen the event and risk attracting some ill-fitting participants – which may damage the value for other participants.
- Where there are specific clients (or prospective clients) for whom the event should be particularly relevant and where we have not received any response,

then personalise the invitation further through a follow up e-mail or, best of all, a follow up telephone call.

- Only use the best presenters for the event. Most audiences today are sophisticated and experienced. They recognise the difference between excellence and mediocrity. A mediocre presentation of even the most valuable subject will weaken the impression to your guests – and hence diminish the value that they perceive.

- Check the venue out well in advance (if the event is not to be run on your premises). Walk the room(s) and check out the facilities.

- Get the presentation team together at least one week in advance to rehearse their input and handovers. Make it a full 'dress rehearsal' including AV. Agree the changes that need to be made then schedule a final rehearsal for a day or two before the event.

- Get the team together at least one week before the event to discuss how they will stage manage the whole event – from meeting and greeting until the time that the last guest has left.

- Ensure that each professional is allocated a specific, agreed number of people for whom they will be responsible.

- Ensure that each support professional knows the questions that he / she is going to use as discussion openers with the people he / she will be meeting. If it is likely that most guests will be 'roaming', then each professional should have two or three questions that they 'own' – in order that guests are not bombarded with the same question each time they begin speaking with someone from the firm.

- Get support staff to contact each guest (or his / her secretary) within 48 hours of the commencement of the event to ensure that the final numbers attending are known.

- 'Colour code' badges in some way so that professionals can quickly identify any 'roaming' guests.

- Make sure that the typeface of the name badges is large enough so that those who are long-sighted do not have to lean forward and peer at a guest's chest in order to read his / her name.

- Make the host professionals' badges distinctly different from those of the guests. This is to save potential confusion for the guests.

- Ensure that all of the firm's representatives (speakers, other professionals and support) arrive before any guests.

- Set up all equipment immediately and have a dry run – ensuring that all AV effects work and that sound, lighting and ventilation are all OK.

- After registration, the receptionists should take each guest to their respective host professional, who should be positioned at a specific 'station'. It is the professional's task to ensure that each guest is catered for. The professionals should stay at their 'station'. (If there are breaks then most guests will gravitate back to their original 'station' – allowing for on-going discussion.)

- Keep the guests out of the main presentation room prior to the start. This allows the presenters any final preparation free from interruption and also allows the seating to be adjusted right up until the last minute.

- The professionals should sit in on the event – to understand exactly what went on, which messages seemed to gain greatest audience interest and which guests had specific questions.

- Don't use the event to try to 'sell' to clients and prospective clients. This is not what they came for and this behaviour will discourage them from participating in events in the future.

- Use the discussion time to get a feel for the issues affecting the guests and their organisations (particularly in relation to the event subject).

- Where there are opportunities in the time available to enlighten guests on other issues affecting them, then do so. This will add to the value that they derive from the event. Where the issue needs greater time and effort to explore, then suggest to the guest that you will drop them a line on the subject.

- If there is any seated catering provided then a table plan should be created between the time that the event kicks off and the catering begins.

- Plan for time at the end of the event when the support professionals can share intelligence on what they discussed, and learned from, different guests.

- Ensure that any new intelligence is used to update the firm's database.

- Each support professional should write to each of the guests for whom he / she was responsible on the day. A 'standard' letter is fine but most letters should be tailored with a paragraph or a couple of lines related to subjects that were raised in discussion with them at the event.

- Where there are specific issues that were raised between the guest and the professional that seem to have some substance behind them, a telephone call should be made, seeking to set up a more focused meeting.

Referrals and references from existing clients

Referrals

A few years ago we were doing a lot of business development training work for a long-standing banking client. The managers that we were working with had, as one of their key tasks, to develop new business from new customers. Their customer base was in the mid corporate market and each manager typically managed around 40 to 50 relationships. According to independent research this bank's mid corporate customers were the most satisfied in the UK. This was not a one-off aberration. Quarter by quarter this bank's customers rated their relationship with their bank – and their bank manager – higher than any other bank's customers did.

However, the managers struggled with the task of new business acquisition and most hated the prospect of being asked to 'cold call'. On one of the workshops we asked the participating group three questions. Question one was, "How many relationships do you manage? Please write the number down on a sheet of paper."

Question two was, "Of the number of relationships that you manage, how many customers have you got who are somewhere between being satisfied and highly delighted with the service that you provide? Will you please write the number down below your first number."

Question three was, "Of the second number that you just wrote down, how many of these customers have you proactively asked for a referral or recommendation in the last year? Will you also write that number down?"

A pattern quickly emerged. The first two numbers were very similar – and the independent market research substantiated these estimates. However, the third number was usually zero.

Often clients do not realise that professionals, as part of their role, are responsible for new business development. It simply never occurs to them that a referral to a colleague or some other business associate would be extremely welcomed by their advisor. Why? Because the advisor has never raised the issue with the client.

Professionals regularly tell us, "I wouldn't know what to say or how to say it. I don't want to put my client under any obligation or pressure."

"Let's try this then," we respond. "You are meeting with one of your clients. You have a good relationship with her and you have just completed a project that has gone extremely well. This is the review meeting and the client has just told you how delighted she is with the outcome of the work. At that point you say to her something along the lines of, 'I'm pleased that you're pleased and we look forward to working with you in the future. Also if you think that there are other people in your organisation – or indeed any other business associates – that we should be talking to about our capabilities then I would welcome the introduction'." Given the context, how painful did that feel?

In asking for a referral two things are important. Firstly there is timing. The subject should be raised when the relationship is on a high. Why would any client recommend the mediocre to a colleague or other business associate? Secondly we have to be comfortable with our choice of words. We are never comfortable with any skill that we have not practised and most professionals have never practised asking for a referral. In our workshops we take professionals back to the scenario of the delighted client and tell them to write down what it is that they would say – word for word, in their own words, words that they will be personally comfortable with. We then get them to practise amongst themselves. It is amazing the improvement that can be seen and the confidence that can be gained through three or four articulations during a few minutes practice.

Having sown the seed the client should be left to decide her own response. Some may just nod, acknowledging that they have heard, but no more. Some will actually respond along the lines of, "I know that the people in our Manchester office are not entirely pleased with the advisors they have been using recently. I'll give them a call and ...."

We should never put pressure on our existing clients or make them feel uncomfortable. Raising the subject of referrals in a thoughtful, practised way at the right time should not result in embarrassment on either side. In practice we find that once clients realise that business development is an important role for the professionals with whom they work, some will act as a continual source of introductions for those professionals whose abilities and relationships they value highly.

How do referrals work as a marketing tool in the light of the two keys to marketing effectiveness? The answer is that whilst the person to whom the professional has been referred is unlikely to receive any immediate direct value, what they do receive is tremendous insight into what it is like to work with the professional concerned. The referee has months or perhaps years of real life experience that she can share with the person to whom she is making the recommendation.

References

References work in a similar way. From time to time prospective clients will ask, "Who have you done this kind of work for in the past and can we speak with them?" Rather than scramble around at this point trying to find suitable referees, professionals should create a bank of satisfied clients where they have the explicit up-front agreement that these people will act as reference points. This has been done in commercial markets for decades. IT companies regularly make use of user site visits as a part of their selling process. Prospective customers are taken to installations similar to the one they are considering purchasing. They can see how the installation works and they can question the existing customer directly. Used well it is a powerful proof and these IT businesses work hard to maintain a stream of recognised user sites where the current customers are happy to act as a living testimony.

Recently we lost a pitch to win a new client – very painful but this time a genuine learning experience. The winners had succeeded, at least in part, due to very imaginative use of a client reference. The winning organisation included the Managing Partner of one of their key clients in their presentation team! As well as demonstrating fantastic loyalty, and implying tremendous satisfaction with the work done, just by being there, the client was also able to give 'unbiased' insights into the opportunities, challenges and issues involved in getting the best value from the advisor who was pitching. Very powerful we thought – just a shame we hadn't thought of it first!

Training events

When reading the Nisus Consulting report into FTSE 100 clients' relationships with law firms we were struck by one anecdote that was in the section of the report entitled

'Delivery of Promotional Tools'. A company's General Counsel said, "(A magic circle law firm) who aren't officially on our panel, came in and did an in-house seminar for us. They've been quite proactive in developing that relationship. The seminar was absolutely excellent. As a result they got some work."

Seems like an efficient way of winning the work of one of the country's largest businesses. And why wouldn't it be efficient? It completely exemplifies the two keys for successful marketing directed toward Defined Prospects. Provide value and allow the prospective client to judge what it feels like to work with us.

And yes, it was free! We know that this used to be anathema to many professional firms, and still is to some. Giving away chargeable time is unthinkable. Law firms that think and behave in this way are probably still circling this FTSE 100 giant wondering how they can win some of the work that is available. Keep circling. Keep wondering.

Surgeries

At one client workshop where we were running the Effect of Different Promotional Activities exercise, one participant volunteered, "Surgeries." It was one of those occasions when the facilitator's mind went blank. He'd done this exercise dozens of times previously and nobody had ever shouted out this word. The response therefore was, "What do you mean by surgeries?"

"Well", said Michael who had volunteered the response, "I do most of my work in medical negligence cases. I tend to deal with very specialist and sometimes obscure and difficult cases and I happen to believe that I'm very good at what I do. The trouble is that the medical negligence people that some of our insurer clients and prospects employ tend to think that they can handle these difficult cases themselves. So, when I find the right time I make an offer to the head of claims. I offer to come in for three or four hours and to run a surgery with his medical negligence people looking only at those cases where they feel that they are struggling and could do with fresh insight. No charge. They get a fresh perspective and advice and I get a closer understanding of the cases that they deal with and how they go about dealing with them.

I've found out that what typically happens is that as soon as I have left the premises the claims manager is on the phone asking his team, 'How did the session with Michael go?' Well, like I said, I'm a specialist and I'm good at what I do. So the usual response is, 'Hey, that was a really useful session. That guy is great. Are we working with him? We certainly should be.' I get loads of work off the back of surgeries with both clients and prospective clients."

Deliver value and provide the client with an opportunity to judge what it is like to work with us. Bulls eye? Probably – and also an excellent example of the Trojan Horse tactic that we will examine in the next chapter.

Seeing the light

At a Managing Business Development workshop that we were running not long ago we were coming to the end of the session examining the Nearness to Client Pyramid and the effects of Corporate, Capability and Contact Marketing activities. At this point one senior professional struck his forehead with the palm of his hand. It appeared that something significant had occurred to him.

When asked to share his thoughts Alan said, "I've always believed that it was wrong to give away my professional time. But if I decide to take a client to the races for the day I put this down as business development activity and nobody raises an eyebrow. It's expected. It's just struck me that if I used the same time to carry out some of these Contact Marketing activities that we've been talking about I'd definitely be a more effective business developer. I think that I've suddenly been released!" he concluded with a big grin.

TREAT PROSPECTS LIKE CLIENTS

Having now looked at best practice in how to employ a number of the promotional tools that are at a firm's disposal, it can be seen that there is a single underlying principle that sits behind the two keys to effective marketing directed toward Defined Prospects. That principle is to treat prospects – particularly those identified as Defined Prospects – like clients.

That means thinking about their businesses and the issues they have to face. It means understanding their particular industry. It means investing time to build and develop the relationship. It means being patient. It means thinking about practical ways to emulate for prospective clients the experiences that actual clients have of our firm and us. It means being prepared to provide some time and effort that may not show an immediate payback. It means always trying to deliver value.

Too often firms treat clients and prospective clients differently. After all potential clients have not paid a penny in fees. The focus is not on adding value and acting in the ways described in the last paragraph it is almost entirely on 'how / what could we sell to these people?' – and you don't have to be greedy to look greedy! There is an implicit promise however that once a prospective client offers the firm a real shot at a real opportunity then the prospect will see the firm's true colours. Trouble is, the prospective client has probably made up her mind and the opportunity may never be offered.

RETURN ON INVESTMENT

In the past many professional services firms have invested much time and financial resources in Corporate and Capability Marketing and less in effective Contact

Marketing. In contrast, when you look at how hard the three levels are to measure in terms of effect and outcomes, Contact Marketing (because of its direct and active nature) is the easiest.

This is one of the reasons why firms have difficulty measuring the effectiveness of their marketing expenditure. They are devoting significant resources to what are the most difficult areas to measure. In turn they may also expect results which only Contact Marketing can deliver. Corporate and Capability Marketing do have a strong role to play in building awareness in the client's mind and helping the client to understand exactly what a firm can deliver. However, without Contact Marketing the prospective client is highly unlikely to convert into a live client.

Whilst we are not suggesting that firms halt expenditure on Corporate Marketing, we do recommend that:

- The overall promotional budget is re-examined in respect of how much is dedicated to the three levels of promotional activities.
- Over time, a greater proportion of Corporate Marketing and communications budgets are devoted to Contact Marketing projects and approaches.
- Measurement systems are adjusted (or in some cases introduced) to reflect this change.

We do believe that this will help firms to see a more direct correlation between what they spend on marketing and the new business they win.

ACCELERATING THE PROMOTIONAL APPROACH THROUGH CAMPAIGNS

Hopefully all of the above makes sense. The problem is that many people reading this book have picked it up because they have a short-term problem. There is a need to generate additional fee income and it is clear that the existing client base will not provide it in the short-term future. In particular the firm would dearly love to meet with the Key Defined Prospects that it has identified but these organisations have remained elusive. In short the firm needs to find ways to win work from new clients and that means gaining an audience with them.

We're back to the problem we looked at earlier in this chapter. Why would a prospective client who is being well served by her existing advisors wish to complicate her life by talking with us? The answer hasn't changed. It is because that in every previous interface with our firm she has gained some form of value. So how can we generate lots of value quickly?

One answer is through campaigns, or as they are more accurately called, high focus, high value, high impact campaigns. We will call them campaigns for short. The essence of these types of campaign is as follows:

- These campaigns should be targeted toward specifically identified senior management people within the Defined Prospects that have been identified.

- It is not unusual to target two or more people within a Defined Prospect as often there is no precise information as to who would be the most appropriate recipients of our campaign. On many occasions the campaign may well be of interest to a number of people.

- The campaign should begin with a written communication to the targeted individuals. It should explain clearly what the firm is trying to do (i.e. convince them that your firm is an organisation that would be of value to them to begin dialogue with) and how you intend to raise their interest.

- The campaign should have about five elements.

- The prime consideration for any material that is sent to the targeted individuals should be, "Will this potentially be of genuine value to him / her?" Don't include brochures and overtly promotional material.

- Each intervention should follow no longer than two weeks after the previous one.

- Consider including in the campaign:

  - Books written by our people

  - Papers produced by our people

  - Copies of articles written by our people and published in trade journals

  - Copies of articles (from external authoritative sources) that would probably be of interest to the targeted individuals

  - Interesting and relevant case studies

  - Outputs from proprietary research

  - Market reports

  - Self-scoring questionnaires on particular issues with an offer to analyse the results

- Ensure that some relevant communication accompanies every piece of material sent to targeted individuals. Ensure that each of these communications is specifically tailored to the person concerned. Ensure that each and every accompanying letter is personally hand signed.

- When the final part of the campaign has been executed, write a letter to the individuals concerned. Express the hope that the information you have sent over the past few weeks has been of interest and of value and has given the recipient some idea of 'where we are coming from'.

- State specifically that you will be calling the recipient on a nominated day (within one week) with a view to seeing if it would be appropriate and timely to arrange a face-to-face meeting.

- Make the call! Don't waste the effort that has gone in up to this point.

In our own firm we use a mix of long and short term marketing activities to attract Defined Prospects into dialogue. Last year we looked at our top 15 fee-producing clients and discovered that eight of them had originally entered into discussions with us primarily as a result of campaigns directed toward senior decision makers. However, we are also aware that the proprietary benchmarking research that we carry out, the articles that we write, the workshops that we run and the word of mouth referrals and recommendations that we foster all provide a supporting environment for these highly targeted campaigns.

To provide some feel for what a campaign could look like we have taken an example of one that we have found to be quite successful. By successful we mean that we will obtain a business meeting with someone that we have targeted in more than 50% of the Defined Prospects included in the campaign.

Week 1	Initial letter accompanied by book – *Creating New Clients*
Week 2	Letter with article on Cross-selling
Week 3	Letter with article on Running Effective Seminars
Week 4	Letter with article – A Measured View of Clients
Week 5	Letter accompanied by book – *Managing Key Clients*
Week 6	Letter with two articles –
	Teaching Smart People How to Learn
	Making Sales Training Work
Week 7	Follow up telephone calls

Someone once said to us, "That seems intense to the point of stalking!." That is not our experience. Occasionally we have a secretary call us and tell us that her boss is not the right person to direct this information to. That's about as negative as it gets. We get many more calls from recipients who, before the campaign is completed, ask to meet with us.

The key is delivering value and the biggest hurdle we have found when firms in need of short-term new business wins seek to implement a campaign approach is that there can be a dearth of material that is likely to provide value. There is then a huge temptation to slip in some overtly 'push' promotional material. Perhaps a brochure or a service flyer. The high focus, high value, high impact campaign has then become devalued to just another mailshot.

Also it should be borne in mind that this is not a silver bullet. Not every Defined Prospect that is campaigned to will want to meet with our firm at that point in time. At PACE we are delighted with a two in three conversion rate of campaigns to meetings. Also this meeting provides us with just the very first step into the P3 section of The PACE Pipeline – the Projecting phase. There could be a long way to go but the campaign has succeeded in getting the people that we want to talk with, to want to talk with us.

GUIDANCE FROM CLIENTS

The Nisus Consulting research looks exclusively into the relationships between lawyers and their clients and we cannot necessarily extrapolate all of the conclusions and apply them to other professional services providers. However, the following quotation from one of the research reports rang true with us and has rung true with clients of other types of professional advisors when we have discussed this subject with them.

"In addressing how they should be approached, a lot of the interviewees chose to start by explaining how they should not be approached. Cold calling, generic letters and brochures came top of this list. Respondents were vexed by the number of uninformed approaches they received from firms which simply said they wanted to be considered for work and when was the next panel review? The consensus was that those who did make an approach should do so in writing, they need to have done their research, worked out their offer and built-in their distinctive benefits. Having done this they should seek a one-to-one meeting. They should not be too pushy."

WHERE TO GO FROM HERE

Where to go from here if you run a firm or have overall responsibility for marketing and business development

Ask your marketing department and / or the individual parts of your firm that are involved in marketing to provide you with a breakdown of last year's promotional activity and (where possible) the spend – broken down into Corporate, Capability and Contact Marketing.

On the basis of this analysis, decide whether the breakdown reflects what the firm should be trying to achieve through its promotional efforts. What changes should be made going into the future based on who your firm is targeting?

Provide guidance to your marketing people, and the practice areas that are involved in their own marketing, as to how you wish to see the balance of promotional activity in the future. Agree objectives with them and measure ongoing performance.

Where to go from here if you run a business unit within a professional firm

Carry out your own analysis on your business unit's promotional activity for the last year – broken down into Corporate, Capability and Contact Marketing. Reflect on why you did what you did – and what were the results?

Based on this analysis, ensure that your business unit has a plan for next year that reflects the balance of activities that will assist you in achieving your unit's fee income objectives.

If you don't do so already, start to measure the Contact Marketing activity expended by each of your fee-earners who have business development responsibility.

If you have a need to generate new client income in the next few months, work with a group of your most interested people to generate the first of your high focus, high value, high impact campaigns and direct this toward a selected group of your Key Defined Prospects.

Where to go from here if you are a marketing or business development professional working with fee-earners

Agree with the fee-earners who they are attempting to influence through promotional activities. Also ensure that there is clarity about the issues that face these clients and Defined Prospects – otherwise any promotional effort or activity risks missing the mark.

If you are having trouble getting professionals to see what their contribution to marketing activities should be, then run The Effect of Different Promotional Activities exercise with them – or alternatively get someone neutral to run this for you.

On the basis of the outcome of this exercise, agree with the fee-earners that you work with the overall shape of the promotional activities that should be focused upon over the next period or next year.

Make an effort to know where you can lay your hands on the kinds of material that could be utilised in a high focus, high value, high impact campaign. The idea is often readily accepted by fee-earners but can stumble in implementation if the right collateral material cannot be found to generate the campaign.

If, in the execution of a campaign, you create new collateral material then share this and make it available to others in the firm.

If you believe that that you and the fee-earners with whom you work can put together a campaign then volunteer to act as the coordinator of this approach.

Where to go from here if you are an individual practitioner within a professional firm

Make a list of the Contact Marketing activities that you could or should get involved in, in your role.

Now take your diary and plan for the next three to four months those specific Contact Marketing activities that you will participate in. Your firm's, your practice area's or your own efforts could generate these opportunities. Make these a priority and fit fee-earning work and other activities around these events.

Chapter 4   **Projecting**

OUTCOMES OF FIRST MEETINGS

As we explained in Chapter 1 when we looked at each of the activities that are needed to build a pipeline of future work, an initial meeting with a Defined Prospect has three potential outcomes. One outcome is that we decide that the prospect is not worth further pursuit. The second is that further pursuit is desirable but there are no immediate opportunities in sight therefore we will have to maintain contact through on-going marketing activities plus e-mail and telephone. The third is that we see an opportunity for work in either the short or medium term and we believe that it is appropriate to begin pursuit of this opportunity.

It is the evidence that we gather at the very first meeting that we have with a Defined Prospect that allows us to make the right decision as to the best way forward. This meeting is therefore critical. It is critical for another reason as well. In our first paragraph we have been very self-centric – *we* will make the decision as to the way that *we* will proceed. There is a danger that we may forget one other important party – the prospective client. She may have something to say about the way forward. Just as we are forming a picture that will allow us to make a decision as to the best way ahead for us, so also is the client. Just like us the prospect is gathering evidence from the very outset – from the very first handshake in the reception area.

As the meeting progresses the prospective client can come to a number of conclusions. For example she may conclude:
- These people seem OK so far so I will tell them about immediate work that they may be able to pitch for. They could be another string to the bow but I won't do anything to enhance their chances over anyone else that I'm talking with.
- These people have really impressed me so far so I will tell them about immediate work that they may be able to pitch for. I'll give them a really good brief and be very open as I have an early feeling that they may be good to work with at some point.
- These people have impressed me but we have nothing on the horizon in the areas that they appear to work in, however I would have no objection to keeping in touch.
- These people are unimpressive and don't measure up to the kind of advisors that we are using today. Even if we have work that their firm could do I don't want to become involved in a discussion with them about it.

Quite clearly we want to make the kind of impression that leads a client to thinking the second option and never considering the fourth.

MANAGING THE FIRST MEETING

Our marketing and follow up has done its job. The Defined Prospect has agreed to a first meeting. A chance now to sell our services! Let's think what may be appropriate. What would they be most interested in? We should start by telling them about … Stop!!

This is where so many professionals go wrong. They see this meeting as a selling opportunity (right) and therefore their job is to pitch to the prospect in order to convince her that their firm has the services and capabilities that she should use in the future – wrong!

Let's look at it from the Defined Prospect's point of view. She has been on the receiving end of our marketing activities and campaigns over a period of time. One or two things made an early impression so she continued to notice our stuff. She thought that a lot of it was good and mostly it was relevant to her. She then received an intensive campaign and could deduce easily that we were a firm that wanted to make a big impression and that clearly wanted to take the discussion further. When we called her up she said that, based on what she had seen to date, she was open to an exploratory meeting but that we had to realise that she used other advisors for the kinds of work that she understood that we did. We said, "Fine, we would expect that, but let's meet anyway." She said, "OK."

Let's also think what will be in the client's mind the day she decides (hopefully) to appoint our firm to carry out the first piece of work for her. She will have reached the point where she is thinking, "I believe I trust these people with this case and I think my organisation and I can work with them." Now, the simple fact is that most people do not reach this conclusion at the end of a one hour meeting, no matter how well we have managed it. And let's not run away with the idea that handling this type of meeting is something that any professional could do easily. After all don't professionals manage all sorts of meetings all of the time?

On this subject we are reminded of some feedback that we saw quite recently. The firm in question employed a person whose responsibilities embraced some of those that we will examine in Chapter 8 when we look at the role of the Business Development Manager. As part of his role he was responsible for getting feedback from clients and prospective clients on pitches and proposals that his firm had either won or lost. This is his feedback, elicited from one prospective client and given to the professional responsible for pitching to that client.

"I firstly asked the client why they had asked us to pitch. I was told that it was because of our 'name and reputation'. In addition they had asked [competitor] to pitch, and they were the ones that won.

The first impressions at the pre-pitch meeting were not very good. I'm afraid that they'd decided against you right from the start because of your performance. Whilst they felt that Jane was somewhat more credible they saw Jonathon as being 'thin' and he came across as 'distant' – as though he had his mind on more important things. They also felt that the team:

- Didn't really understand their organisation and hadn't researched them before you showed up
- Didn't really listen to what they had to say
- Asked and then answered your own questions

Of the proposal document that you sent they felt that this was far too general, full of standards and technicalities and in no way specific to their organisation's needs. They were looking for a much more focused and specific report.

When it came to the presentation they were really disappointed. They felt that the team was inappropriate given the nature of the proposed work and the nature of the people that they would be working with. The team members were seen as insufficiently experienced and lacking in 'grey hair'. Whilst the competitors also didn't do well at the presentation they had a couple of more heavyweight partners on their team and this went down better with the board / management team. They said that both ours and our competitor's presentation skills were 'awful' and wondered if this had something to do with lawyers in general. They said that the presentations were dull and uninteresting and that we in particular made too many incorrect assumptions."

The proposal and presentation, poor as they were, were a total waste of time and effort. The impression made on the client at the first meeting had, in fact, been decisive.

It appears that some professionals struggle to impress in these early meetings.

Building trust through demonstrating competence, credibility and compatibility

So how do we get a prospective client to the point where she says, "I trust you and want to work with you and your firm?

1   Firstly we must accept that (except in unusual circumstances) this feeling will never be created within a prospective client in just one meeting. The number of contacts required is indeterminate. It will depend on the nature of the client

and the nature of the type of work that we are trying to win. The more 'mission critical' the work or the more it impacts personally on the people giving the instructions the longer the process is likely to take, as there is greater level of trust that needs to be developed.

2   Secondly we create trust by demonstrating to the client over a period of time that we have *competence* and *credibility* and that we are *compatible* with her and her business.

Competence

The client deduces our competence by gaining a feel for how much we know about our area of expertise – and how much we know about her type of business and the market conditions in which it operates. She also gains a feel for our competence by our references to previous relevant experiences. Even more importantly she develops an understanding of our competence when we are able to use our knowledge and track record and project this onto her situation – demonstrating real expertise.

Perhaps small wonder then that many professionals are so tempted in a first meeting to convince the prospective client of their knowledge, track record and expertise.

Credibility

Credibility in the client's eyes is built through a number of experiences. People who lack confidence have trouble in building a credible image. Some professionals struggle with this. In their professional environment they may have ample confidence but when faced with a 'selling' meeting this confidence can be left in the car park. There is no point in telling a prospective client, "Don't worry if I come across as a bit flustered and not knowing what I'm doing in this meeting because when you engage my services you'll find I'm a great technician." Maybe it's a failing of clients but they usually find it difficult to separate the two people who share the same suit! They make their judgements on a person's credibility by what they see and hear – whatever the role the professional may be playing at the time.

And prospective clients are quick to make early judgements. Why shouldn't they be? Most of us are the same. The first five minutes of a first meeting are critical. The prospect reaches a lot of interim conclusions very quickly. How comfortable and confident does this person appear to be? How organised is he? How much does he seem to know about what he is doing? What are his social graces like? Can he outline succinctly what he sees as the purpose of the meeting? How much is he interested in me and my agenda – or is he just interested in trying to plough a furrow he's decided in advance? All the telltale signs will be there in the first few minutes and we can be sure that the client will be picking up and interpreting these signs subliminally. Therefore to build credibility a professional needs to know exactly how to open one of these meetings – to know exactly what behaviours to demonstrate.

Over time professionals can also build their credibility by demonstrating two other important behaviours. Number one is honesty and number two is delivering as promised.

Adopting a selling hat does not give professionals licence to behave in the way that archetypal salespeople are portrayed – telling the customer whatever is necessary in order to get them to sign on the bottom line. The vast majority of professionals have an excellent grasp of honesty and honest behaviour as it relates to their professional role. All we are suggesting is that they extend this ethos into their business development activities and never exaggerate or hide an unpalatable fact from a prospective client. The sad fact is that if we are discovered to have knowingly vocalised an untruth then our credibility in the eyes of the Defined Prospect has gone – and so has any trust.

If the selling process is extended over a period of time – as our experience shows that it will be in most occasions – there are ample opportunities for the client to gain first hand experience of our ability to deliver as we have promised. "I'll get back to you on that tomorrow", is easy to say but if in hindsight it is not something important, does it really matter if we don't get back until the day after tomorrow? It's not important providing the prospect isn't keeping count – but mostly they are. The prospect is weighing up all the evidence that she experiences that will indicate whether or not we would be suitable advisors to work alongside at some point in the future. She will judge what it is like to work with us by how we are 'selling' to her.

Compatibility

If a professional is really interested in demonstrating compatibility to a prospective client then he will be adaptable and adjust the way he behaves. For instance if the client's nature is to be a little laid back and measured, then the professional should rein in his natural brisk approach and adopt a pace somewhat more akin to that of the prospect. It is human nature for people to like to do business with people they like – and the people that we most easily get on with are people rather like ourselves. There is no suggestion of professionals having to change their personalities. That is nonsense. It is a case of having the interest and desire to observe carefully how others behave and, if necessary, temporarily adjust our own behaviour.

Demonstrating real interest in the client is crucial. Whilst most clients recognise that they need dispassionate, objective advice from their advisors, by the same token they would also like to deal with people that they believe are committed to them, their business and their cause. Good new business developers are curious. They ask lots of questions and don't accept answers at face value. They dig further to ensure that they *really* understand. This questioning gives the prospect evidence that this advisor is *really* interested – he wants to know all about her business, the things that her part of the organisation gets involved in and about her and her role. He wants to understand her past experiences, what good looks like through her eyes and what she is seeking in the future. He shows that he is more interested in hearing her opinions than voicing his own.

Linked to being an excellent questioner, a professional who can build compatibility will always be an excellent listener and will have learned the skill of active listening. Active listening is much more than turning our ears up to maximum receptivity or nodding at the right time. It is about giving the prospective client explicit feedback – demonstrating that not only have we understood what the other person has said but that we also understand how they feel about what they have told us. We focus a lot of attention on this skill in *Creating New Clients*.

Compatibility can also be demonstrated by finding small ways to show that we care. For instance we may read in a trade journal that one of the Defined Prospects that we are in dialogue with has won an industry award. Instead of pointing out her picture to a colleague and saying, "I know her!" why don't we drop her a short e-mail congratulating her. If we see an article in a magazine that addresses a subject that we know one of our Defined Prospects has an interest in, then why not take a copy and send it to her with a short note? Simple acts but all too rare. Showing we care is about demonstrating to a prospective client that we are thinking about her and her business even when we are not in her presence.

Finally it is hard to find too much empathy with a person who is never wrong. No matter what, they are invulnerable! Some professionals wear this façade. In respect of professional work it is critical that any fee-earner seeks to be as right and accurate as he can be at all times. This is part of what the client is paying for. However, this invulnerability should not extend to every aspect of a professional's behaviour – particularly in some of the more human contacts. People who portray an image of absolute invulnerability at all times are seldom warm, are usually arrogant and at worst are seen as having Teflon shoulders. It's better to say occasionally, "That was down to me – my fault", than to always claim that shortcomings are due to others. Demonstrating a little vulnerability helps in building compatibility.

This all sounds like a lot of effort. It is – but let us return to our original premise. Our Defined Prospects are other firms' clients. Moreover, if our selection criteria are working well they will be the *key* clients of these other firms. The very best of these competitors may have key client plans in place aimed at building the strength of their relationships month on month, year on year. We are going to have to be very good to win work from these entrenched incumbents and to be very good we are going to have to put in a lot of effort. And as a famous man once said, "The greatest opportunities in life come disguised as hard work."

This takes us back to the concept that we introduced in the previous chapter – we need to treat prospects like clients.

Structuring the First Meeting

Let us assume that we have agreed with the Defined Prospect that for our first meeting we need an hour. Our experience tells us that most prospective clients are unwilling to give more than an hour to an initial exploratory meeting. The exception to this is where the advisor comes with a strong recommendation from someone for whom the prospect has high regard.

How should this hour ideally be used? The hour should follow the PACES process and should be split roughly as shown below. Assume that the meeting starts on the hour.

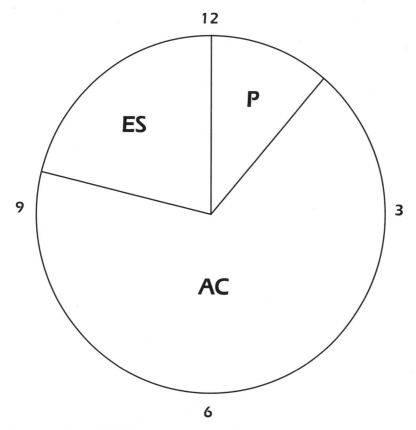

The elements of the PACES process are as follows.

P   Position ourselves and our organisation

A   Ascertain in detail the prospective client's situation and requirements

C   Confirm to the prospect our understanding of their situation and requirements

E   Explain or explore a suitable way forward – based on what has gone before in the meeting

S   Seek commitment to the suggested way forward

'P'

The 'P' part of the meeting is the first five minutes referred to earlier. In reality this can extend to seven or eight minutes but should never be allowed to go on any longer than ten. In these few minutes we are introducing the firm and ourselves, setting the scene and agreeing the purpose and direction of the meeting with the prospective client.

'AC'

The 'AC' part of the meeting should take up the bulk of the time available. It is in this part of the meeting that we are building an understanding of the Defined Prospect's business today, where it is going in the future and the kind of requirements that she may have of professional firms like our own. We are trying to create a picture in our own mind of the prospect's needs and wants. We are also developing a feeling as to whether this client and the type of work that she is looking for in the future from firms like ours fits with our aspirations and strengths.

If it looks like this is a relationship that we want to take forward we are also trying to gain information that will enable us to progress our business development activities in the most effective way.

In this phase of the meeting we are listening to the prospective client and prompting her with questions some of which we have prepared prior to the meeting. Not only are we listening but we are actively listening – meaning that we are not coming to conclusions about what we have been told until we have checked our understanding with the prospect. Yes, all this in about 40 minutes!

'ES'

On the assumption that what we have learned to this point has whetted our appetite to take the relationship further, in the last ten to 15 minutes of the meeting we should:
- Give the prospective client two or three really cogent arguments as to why our firm may be of value to her in the future – based not on generic arguments but related back directly to what we have been told over the past 40 minutes or so.
- Suggest a way ahead – or put a couple of alternatives forward for the client to choose from. These suggestions should meet three criteria. Firstly, they should not be difficult for the prospective client to agree to. Secondly, they should involve the prospect in some form of action – even if it is simply to meet again. Thirdly, they should in some way keep us in direct face-to-face contact with the client and her organisation.
- Gain agreement to the suggested way forward.

In *Creating New Clients* we go into considerable depth exploring the skills involved in executing each of these stages of the initial meeting.

PROPOSALS

Timing

On some occasions the very first meeting with a Defined Prospect will involve discussion about a piece of work that appears to be within the remit and capability of the firm. The AC part of the meeting is very productive for the professional concerned as he probes to find out exactly what the work is and what support the client is looking for from her advisors. In the ES phase of the meeting the professional, based on what he has heard, states why he believes that his firm is well placed to help the client on this occasion and provides examples and offers references to back his assertions.

And then ...... there is a slight pause. The meeting is down to the last five minutes. We're at the time when (the professional wrongly believes) if he were a salesman, he would 'close'. Instead he says, "Why don't I send you a proposal?"

"Great", says the prospect, "that's just what I was about to suggest." Yes, if the professional could have held the pause for only a moment longer the prospective client would have asked him for a proposal. She clearly wants a proposal from him. Both parties, greatly relieved that the awkward little silence has been overcome, smile with satisfaction at a mutually agreeable way forward.

The professional then says, "I should be able to get the proposal to you by Wednesday next week. Will that be OK?"

"That's perfectly OK", replies the client, "there is no particular rush."

By burning the midnight oil and getting his secretary to work overtime the proposal is posted to the prospect on Tuesday evening and arrives on her desk on Wednesday morning. She is not there to receive it as she is in Brussels that day on business and won't be back in the office until Friday. When she returns on Friday her day is filled with meetings. She sees the thick proposal and puts it into her in-tray with the intention of reading it when she has time.

Three weeks later, having heard nothing, the professional decides to give the prospect a call to find out how she feels about his proposal. The call is taken by the prospect's secretary, who briefly puts him on hold and asks her boss if she wants to take the call. The prospect glances guiltily at the proposal still sitting in her in-tray and says to her secretary, "Tell him that I'm in a meeting but that I will get back to him." The first part of the statement is untrue but she has the honest intention of fulfilling the second part.

A week later the prospect realises that it is starting to get close to the time when she will need to make a decision as to whom she will appoint as her professional advisor for the upcoming initiative. She puts time aside in her diary to read the proposal undisturbed. The written document is OK. It is a bit generic in parts but then it was based on only one discussion. It's also quite weighty – which is one of the reasons that it has remained unread for so long. When the professional wasn't sure he opted for detail rather than brevity.

In her mind's eye she tries to bring into focus the face of the professional but she fails. It was nearly a month ago and the week following that meeting she must have met at least 40 new faces during her Brussels trip alone. She recalls that the meeting with the professional seemed to go quite well but the details are very hazy.

With the initiative now firmly on her immediate agenda she picks up the telephone and calls her regular advisor. At the time of calling she thinks, "Why am I calling him? He should be calling me from time to time, but it seems he disappears after each piece of work is concluded." However, she reflects that he is a very safe pair of hands, he knows her organisation and he works well in coordination with her internal team.

A meeting is arranged and this advisor is briefed on the initiative and the work that is required. After clarifying the details of what is needed the advisor asks the client what she needs from him.

"An outline proposal", she replies "four or five pages at the most", (thinking about the hour and a half it took to wade through the first proposal). I know that you can do the work. I really need a schedule of how you would tackle the work, the resources that you would use from both your side and mine and an estimate of costs."

"When do you need it by?" asks the advisor.

"I know it's a bit of a rush but could I have it by Friday, I need to make a decision. Oh, and by the way I'm also looking at someone else for this work."

The advisor weighs up the words and the tone and concludes that in reality this is a one horse race. He can only lose if he falls over and breaks a leg.

A week later the prospect (feeling extremely guilty) picks up the telephone and calls the first professional. She apologises profusely for the time it has taken to get back to him but there were unexpected delays. She thanks him for his proposal and comments on its thoroughness but regretfully has to inform him that on this occasion the company chose another advisor.

"Were we too expensive?" asks the professional, revealing his biggest fear and the factor that he believes is the main reason his firm does not win more new work.

"No", replies the client, "it wasn't an issue of money." As she replies she reflects that whilst her current advisor had clearly made an effort to keep the overall fees down, probably due to the fact that he knew this was a competitive situation, he was still more than 10% more expensive than the first proposal. "We just felt that on this occasion another firm met our needs better."

After the call the professional reviews his meeting notes and the proposal. The proposal is a work of art. It is truly excellent. It covered everything.

"Another client who doesn't know what she's looking for," he concludes.

Flawed logic

When pursuing new work from new clients many professionals are following a flawed logic. It goes something like this. We know from our dealings with clients whom we know well that before they make a decision as to who they will use for a certain piece of work, that they will need a proposal. The proposal (and sometimes a presentation or pitch to support it) come just before the client makes a decision. In our previous scenario the second advisor's experience would support this line of thinking. One usually closely follows the other. The logic is sound up to this point. The observations are correct.

The thinking continues therefore that, when one is pursuing new work, one objective is to get to the proposal stage as soon as possible as this will mean that the client will make a decision (hopefully a positive one) in the near future. Now we're hopelessly off track.

Over the years we have been asked on numerous occasions by clients and prospective clients, "Do you run courses on proposal writing?" We learned a long time ago to answer this question with a question such as, "Why, what is the issue?" Almost always the issue is that the firm in question believes that they are not converting enough of their proposals into work. They may tell us "Our conversion rate has slipped to one in eight."

It may be worth digressing at this point to comment on conversion rates. A one in eight conversion rate is meaningless. If a firm wishes to measure proposal conversion rates it must measure five separate conversion rates. These are:
- Proposals for extensions of existing work and projects.
- New work of the same type that we have carried out for a client in the past.
- New work that we have never carried out previously for the client.
- New work (by definition) for a prospective client where we have proactively identified the opportunity.
- New work for a prospective client where they have approached us to bid.

One in eight does not begin to provide a clue as to where the issue lies.

If the client and our estimate of the potential work warrant it, we will usually suggest an alternative way forward. Rather than quote them for a training course we are willing to come in for a day, spend some time looking at some typical proposals, talk with the people who composed them and try to understand the context in which these proposals were constructed. We agree that once we have concluded our investigations we will meet with the client again to give our feedback. How much will this cost? Nothing usually!

It is interesting to meet the people who buck the trend. Not everyone in our troubled prospective client converts one in eight proposals into work. Some perform far worse. Some perform far better. Some win two in three. We have found that when you ask these people their secret, the essence of their reply is as follows. "Unless I simply cannot avoid it, I never write a proposal unless I know that I've got the work."

We have never found a case where the proposal problem has solely been the quality of the written documentation, nor a case where this was the prime contributor to the lack of success. What almost inevitably sits behind the issue is a flawed selling process. A proposal on its own cannot win work for a firm. It can only lose it. As David Maister wrote in his chapter entitled *How Clients Choose* in his book *Managing the Professional Services Firm*: "The vast majority of professional projects are awarded at the pre-proposal stage: the formal proposal and / or presentation merely confirm (or destroy) a decision already made. If you can't afford to spend time, up-front, don't bother writing the proposal."

One of our aims in talking in further depth with the people in a firm that has a 'proposal problem' business is to understand where the flaws occur.

TAKING THE SELLING PROCESS FORWARD

In the PACES process the 'E' part is 'Explain or explore a suitable way forward'. Hopefully we have killed off the idea that a proposal is a good way forward after a first meeting. So how do we conclude what is a good way forward to which we would like our Defined Prospect to commit? Some information would be useful to help us decide.

An example

Let us take an example of part of the 'AC' phase of a meeting. This meeting is between a Human Resources (HR) consultant and a prospective client who is the HR Director of a business. The discussion up to this point has been about the business's need for help in introducing an appraisal system – creating the system and training people in its implementation and use. The prospective client's requirements seem to have been quite well explored up to this point.

Consultant	It's clear then that you've decided that you need outside assistance with this project. Can you tell me, when it comes to the final decision and you are perhaps looking at the proposals of, say, a shortlist of three or four organisations, what will be the critical criteria that you will use in order to reach your decision as to whom you will appoint?
Client	Experience and track record will be vital. We will want to know that the firm concerned has carried out very similar work in a number of businesses that are very like our own. We'd want references to this effect. People that we can talk to. Also we would want the people

who are working on our project to be those individuals that have had that previous relevant experience and success. And of course we would be looking for value for money.

Consultant   I'd like to come back to that, but what about your team? You've mentioned them on a few occasions? What do you think that they would be looking for in the people that you choose to work with?

Client   Again I believe that they would be looking for relevant experience but also for people with whom they feel they have good chemistry. In addition the consultant's team should be mixed, men and women, to reflect the mix that we have here.

Consultant   OK. That's useful to know. And what about you, you personally? What are you looking for?

Client   Well I know this is going to be a big project and it will involve a lot of change but as I said earlier we do have something of a process here already. If there are parts of it that we can incorporate into the new appraisal process then I would like to do that. When the consultants are gone it will be me and my people who have to keep the organisation enthused about the value of the new appraisal process and the more we make it totally new and different the more difficult that task will become.

Consultant   So you clearly don't want change for change's sake and wherever possible the new process should integrate with the old – if that can be achieved.

Client   Right on the nail.

Consultant   You said earlier that you were looking for value for money. Now, when we approach projects like this we can tackle them in different ways. One decision we need to make is about how much we use your people and how much we use our own.

One key factor that would help us to shape our proposal with regard to the mix of resources to employ would be the budget that you are thinking of allocating to the project. Can you give me any rough guide to what you are considering?

Client   I don't really want to talk specific sums but I can see why you need an idea. The number is around six figures.

Consultant   £100,000?

Client	Of that order – a little more.
Consultant	That's fine. That gives me a feel. What does that budget cover?
Client	Everything. From inception to going live. That includes the agreed process and documentation for all the major departments that I spoke of earlier across all of our sites in this country plus the two in Germany and the one in France. The IT obviously has to be included plus translation.
Consultant	Do you have people who could do that translation work?
Client	That would be simple for us.
Consultant	Good. We could look to reduce some costs there then. You didn't mention training. What about training?
Client	No, that comes from a separate budget. Again we've allocated some money here, but this is an area where I would like to make more use of some of my people.
Consultant	So a train-the-trainer approach may be an appropriate part of the solution?
Client	I hadn't really thought about it in those terms but yes, you're probably right.
Consultant	When do you want the new appraisal process up and running?
Client	We'll miss the next round of appraisals – such as they are today. They're meant to happen in a couple of month's time. However I'd like to have the new system running for the next time – which is October next year.
Consultant	So therefore the training we spoke about will have to happen in August and September and the train-the-trainer (if we go that route) would need to happen in July. Allow say three months for the design and implementation with all the necessary documentation and IT element and that brings us back to April. Does that sound right?
Client	It does but April is a bad month for us. It's our year end. We couldn't give this project much of our attention in April.
Consultant	OK. That means a March start with a hiatus in April then. I guess that whoever you work with is going to need four to six weeks probably to

release the right people for the work. That brings us back to early February-ish. When were you thinking of appointing your advisors?

Client   We hadn't decided on a specific date but working on that kind of schedule we will have to make a decision by the middle of January. There is a board meeting on Friday the 19th so we'd need to have decided a week before that in order that I can advise the board of what we are doing and whom we are working with.

Consultant   It's the 15th of November today, so what will happen in your organisation between now and 12th of January with regard to taking forward this project and coming to a decision as to who you will work with?

Client   We need to speak further with our Divisional Directors and flag up that this new appraisal process is now definitely on the way. We've been talking about it for some time and I'm concerned that they may think that this is just more talk and that they won't be ready for the commitment needed – particularly when we get to the implementation and training stages. I'd also like to get a couple of them to be part of the selection process, even if this only means attending the presentations of the short list. They can be a prickly lot so I'd like to get them involved.

Consultant   So you are looking for a presentation?

Client   We're planning to talk with about half a dozen consultancies like yourselves and invite a number who seem to talk sense to make a proposal. That might be two or three. It could conceivably be six, but that's unlikely. On the basis of the written documents we will then invite some or all of these firms to make a presentation, using the people whom it is proposed would work with us. We will need to schedule these presentations for the 10th and 11th I guess, which means that we will need the proposals for the first day back in January, which is the 3rd.

Consultant   You mentioned getting a couple of the Divisional Directors involved in the presentation. Who else would you like to involve in the process?

Client   I wouldn't make the decision without also involving a couple of my people who will be heavily involved in the programme. I want to get my HR Manager and my Director of Training, who are both based here, involved in some way or another – at least at the proposal and presentation stages.

Consultant	You mentioned it earlier, so you'd probably expect me to ask. Who else is making up the six that you're talking with?
Client	I'd expect you to ask but I'm not telling you.
Consultant	Can I ask if they're people that you've worked with before?
Client	They're not. We don't make use of HR consultants very often. The people that we're talking with, like yourselves are the kinds of names that you would recognise for this kind of work.
Consultant	That's fine. Just let me confirm again that we are very interested in working with you on this project and I hope that from what I told you earlier of our capabilities and past experience that we will be one of the firms that you invite to propose for this work.
Client	I think that on the basis of this meeting you are safe to assume that we will be asking you to propose.
Consultant	Thank you. Can I suggest a way forward? A while back you said that you were anxious not to reinvent too many wheels – that if part of today's processes could be incorporated into the future appraisal system that this would be advantageous as it would make your life somewhat easier.
Client	That's right.
Consultant	What I am proposing is that a colleague and I spend, say, half a day looking at exactly what you have in place now – the system and the documentation. Perhaps your HR Manager could provide us with a 'guided tour' of what you have now. If we could then spend a couple of hours by ourselves we could formulate our thoughts. Following that, if we could then meet with you for say 30 or 40 minutes we could give you our opinion of where the links could be between what you have today and what you are likely to have in the future. I believe that there would be benefits for both parties here.
	This exercise would be helpful for us in putting together our proposal in a way that really fits your situation. I also believe that it would give you an early indication of the level of change that you may be introducing – allowing you to prepare your ground accordingly. Does that sound sensible?
Client	Before I say yes, how much will this cost?
Consultant	Nothing. We view this as part of our due diligence needed to construct our proposal but I am sure that you will derive benefit from the exercise as well.

Client	I'm comfortable with that. I'll speak with my HR Manager and we'll put a date in the diary and organise the day accordingly.
Consultant	If it is possible it would also be useful to spend some time with your Director of Training. It would be really helpful to know how he sees his resources in respect of carrying out appraisals skills training. Once we have a feel for his situation we could also give him some ideas based on our experience in similar situations. Again it's about integrating our approach with the real on-the-ground situation.
Client	OK. We'll try to find a day when they are both available sometime in the next couple of weeks.
Consultant	That would be ideal.

The Value of Commercial Qualification

The discussion above is an example of what is called 'Commercial Qualification' of an opportunity. As the opportunity emerges in the meeting the professional gets a feel for how interesting it is to his firm. It could be interesting for two reasons. Firstly the size of the fee income may make the opportunity interesting. A word of caution here though. The very first piece of work won from a new client is rarely large and if we find ourselves competing for a substantial opportunity against known, proven entities the odds are against our winning. As we pointed out previously, to make a decision in our favour is asking the client to take a big risk.

The second reason that the opportunity could be interesting is that the piece of work on offer may not be large but it may be the entrée into a client that the firm wants to establish a relationship with. Therefore we may be willing to invest disproportionately more in winning the work in order to gain this initial foothold.

The professional wants to find out if there are particular issues that will predicate against his firm's bid for the work or if there are any particular advantages that his firm has that they should seek to exploit. He also wants to know how to position the main thrust of his proposal. He therefore asks a series of questions that are aimed at establishing **the bases of decision.** How will you decide? What factors are important to you and your team?

The professional also wants to establish if the money that the prospective client has in mind is in line with the work and the results she is expecting. Clients are often coy about this subject. The client in our example was less than forthcoming on this subject. Therefore we have to give clients and prospective clients a good reason why it is *in their interests* to provide us with some idea of the money they have to allocate and what they are expecting for this money. Some clients will never tell us their budgetary or fee expectations. The only 'crime' is not to try to find out.

A participant on one of our workshops who worked for a technology consultancy told us of a piece of work that they had recently bid for. They had had one briefing meeting (at which the subject of money was never raised) and then went back to make a presentation. When they got to the subject of fees they quoted the client just over £100,000 for the initial piece of work. The client's people were stunned! When asked at this point what they had in mind, the reply was £5,000! What amazed us even more was that the consultancy then went back and revised their proposal to £5,000 and the client went ahead with them. Mostly we never get a second chance in situations like this and we are still trying to figure out why the client accepted the second proposal. Regardless, the lesson is that we need to try to understand the **budgets and money** angle.

If at this point the professional is still interested in the opportunity and believes that his firm has a realistic chance of winning, he needs to establish the **timescales** involved. We continue to be surprised by how many clients have a clear view of what they need but have not thought through the timescales. The consultant in our example worked through the timescales in a way that we would recommend. Start by establishing when the client wants the final outcome, then work back from there. That way both parties can agree what time is available between the meeting in which they are engaged and the decision date. Also the client gets an early feel for the likely time that will be required to execute the work in question. Unrealistic expectations can be dealt with very early on.

By this stage the professional is beginning to think of ways that he may best utilise the time between this meeting and the decision date.

However, before he makes any suggestions, the professional needs to understand the likely **decision making process** on the client's side. What will happen on the client's side of the fence over the time period between now and the decision date? Who will get involved and what will their involvement be? Too often professionals pursuing a bid become obsessed with their sales process and forget entirely that that is irrelevant.

What is critical is to understand *the client's buying process*. The real professional knows that he has to tie his whole approach into this if he is to be successful. To ignore it is folly.

As a final raincheck the professional will wish to find out about **alternatives, competitors and incumbents.** In the example above the consultant had presumably, from his earlier questioning, established that this is a real project and that the client is going to need the help of external advisors. Other alternatives are out of the question. He mostly drew a blank on his question about competitors but he will probably conclude that he is up against mainstream organisations and not niche players. The really good news is that it appears that no competitor has that immense advantage of being the incumbent trusted advisor.

It appears at this point that it is a fairly even playing field. Time to change all that.

Once an interesting opportunity has come to light, Commercial Qualification is about understanding:

- The bases of decision – both corporate and personal
- The budgets and money situation
- The timescales
- The decision making process
- The alternatives, competitors and incumbents

'Audience Research'

Neil Flett, who is the author of a book cleverly entitled *Pitch Doctor*, heads up an international consultancy called Rogen. The firm specialises in helping clients to win major pitches – typically pitches where the value of the business is worth six figures or more. Neil and his company found fame in 1993 when they coached the Sydney Olympic Games pitch team (including the Prime Minister of Australia and his Dutch born wife).

Sydney's final presentation in Monte Carlo was stunning and the rest is history. Sydney won the Games and staged the most successful Olympic event of all time. As I sat down to begin reading *Pitch Doctor* I imagined a book packed from front to back on what to do and how to do it in that vital hour or so in front of the client. This wasn't what I found.

According to Flett (and in line with our experiences and conclusions) the critical part of pitching is meeting in advance with the proposed audience for the pitch and finding out what will persuade them toward your solution. He calls this 'audience research' and dedicates great tranches of his book to the subject. To quote Flett from his book, "This is not *an* important part of pitching business – it is *the* important part."

It would be excellent PR and the ultimate accolade for his own business to claim that the brilliant planning, 'choreography' and execution of the final Monte Carlo presentation was the winning element in the Sydney bid. Flett, however, gives huge credit instead to those hard working Australian Olympic bid officials who spent years prior to the final presentation conducting audience research with the IOC delegates who would listen to the final arguments in presentation form and would make the ultimate decision.

Flett's experience has him conclude that "Pitches are won before the presentation – it should be proof that the right choice has been made."

Moving the Goalposts

In one of our clients – who bid for both private and public sector work – the expression 'moving the goalposts' is now part of the firm's language. Everyone understands exactly what it means. In a competitive bid situation one of the questions that the bid team asks of itself is, "What have we done to move the goalposts?" In other words what have we done in order to change the client's initial brief in order to give ourselves an advantage over our competitors? They don't always succeed but it is always part of their bid process and the practice has seen them achieve some stunning wins.

Returning to our HR consultant and his prospective client, by now the consultant is in a position to suggest a way forward. In his mind's eye he can see five people reading his firm's proposal. He can see the same group of five listening to his team's presentation on the 10th or 11th of January. Right now they are strangers. He wants them there as allies. He wants them to read his firm's proposal and be saying to themselves, "That's *exactly* what *I* need." He wants them to greet his team on the day of the presentation with warm smiles and first names.

Now, having carried out his Commercial Qualification, he is in a position to suggest ways to achieve this – ways that will also allow his firm to produce a better proposal and ways that will deliver direct additional benefits to the client as well.

What is likely to be the outcome of the day that the professional and his colleague spend at the client's premises? Firstly they will establish a relationship with two key people involved in the decision making process. They will demonstrate to these people that they want to understand them and their roles in this initiative. The questions that they ask, the way they listen, the way they behave and the comments that they make will demonstrate competence, credibility and compatibility. The ideas that they generate for the HR Director and the Director of Training will add value and be welcomed by these people. They will be allowing these key individuals to come to the conclusion that these are probably the sort of people that they would like to work with.

In the discussions with the HR Manager and the Director of Training, they will start to understand more fully the business's current situation and its particular requirements. It is likely that new dimensions of comprehension will be developed and this greater understanding will generate additional ideas. For instance the HR Manager may be keen to not only have the necessary documentation as agreed with his Director but also a tailored 'how to' manual. This would be a guide to which people can refer before they kick off their round of appraisals, long after they have done their initial skills training in how to conduct appraisals using the company's new process. It's an excellent idea.

The consultant, in his follow up meeting with the HR Director, will run this idea past him. This is something his firm is well qualified to produce as part of its solution. Is this something that the HR Director would like them to include as an additional part of their solution? The answer is yes. The ground is tilting. The goalposts are moving. All competitors that received the initial even playing field briefing will now be meeting an out of date specification.

By the time that second meeting with the HR Director happens, the professional will have found a cogent, value adding reason to meet with a sample of the Divisional

Directors. It would be eminently sensible that these are the two people that the HR Director has in mind to be involved in the appointment decision. If it is impossible to meet with these people then the professional will seek agreement to speak with them over the phone. These discussions demonstrate to the operational people that this consultancy is interested in their views and their issues. And, with any luck, the perspectives gained from these discussions will subtly change the initial brief again and give the consultant additional, differentiated ways of constructing his firm's solution. The goalposts are moved even further.

Bidding for public sector work

In our workshops we have been challenged on many occasions with, "You can't do that in the public sector." Very often, before we have had time to respond, someone in the workshop group has come back with, "Yes you can – let me give you an example ..." The fact is that the rules vary. In the worst case situation the rules state that potential bidders are not allowed to contact those who will be making the appointment decision. The bidders can only respond in writing to the written brief.

[As an aside we believe that organisations that behave in this way take horrendous procurement risks. Anything can hide behind a well written document. And the advisors that guide public sector agencies to adopt this method of procurement should be taken out and shot. After all it's our money that they're spending with their blindfolds on.]

At the other end of the spectrum a senior manager within a large government agency once told us, "If, after receiving our Invitation to Tender (ITT) we were not personally contacted by any organisation we had included, we would write them off. We would assume that if all they could do was to respond by cutting and pasting a proposal they were not really that interested in us."

Seems like the rules and the attitudes are different in different places at different times. It is always worth testing the water. Don't assume the worst case scenario because a competitor may ask the question and steal a march – and the business.

The firm mentioned earlier that sets out to 'move the goalposts' was bidding not long ago for a huge piece of work from a significant local health authority. The work was of an on-going nature and was therefore extremely valuable. The firm made a point of taking every opportunity to get close to its prospective client before it came to the time that a proposal had to be submitted. Through this series of meetings it became evident to them that the firm could substantially improve the delivery of what the health authority were looking for but it did mean submitting a proposal that did not match with the tender document. The firm spoke with the prospective client who quickly saw the merit in their ideas.

The authority agreed that the firm could submit a non-compliant bid providing that they also submitted a compliant bid. What the internal rules of this health authority's procurement were, is uncertain. However, they were the only firm allowed to submit a non-compliant bid. In the end, due to the very size of the business the health authority split the business between two firms. Our client was one of those that walked away with the joint first prize. All this may seem like a lot of work but £400,000 a year is probably worth a little more effort than normal.

THE TROJAN HORSE

The offer by the HR Consultant to spend time with the HR Manager and the Director of Training was a classic implementation of the tactic we call the Trojan Horse. The principles behind the Trojan Horse tactic are:
- It is a gift that provides benefit to the client or prospective client.
- The gift must be clearly and tightly defined and agreed. It is not an open ticket to free advice and services from the firm.
- It allows us to reach parts of the prospective client's organisation and decision making process that we would not otherwise have opportunity to access.
- There must be a *quid pro quo* for us. We must also derive benefit from the activity.

On the first point the HR consultant did not say, "I want to come in and talk to some of the main decision influencers." He gave the client explicit reasons why meeting with these people would deliver benefit to the Director of Training and to the HR Director himself.

Related to the second point the gift was clearly scoped – two people for one day and verbal recommendations emerging from these 'insight' meetings.

Thirdly, the meetings allowed influential contact with two people who otherwise may have remained in the background until the final presentations. Also the interaction would show the consultant and his colleague engaged in something close to their 'working role' – creating the opportunity for the client's people to 'judge what it is like to work with us' – the concept that we introduced in the previous chapter.

Finally, the consultant knew from his previous experience that this investment of time was likely to provide substantial payback.

It is probably clear now why we referred in the previous chapter to Michael's offer of surgeries as a good example of a Trojan Horse. The Trojan Horse can be used as part of our Contact Marketing or it can be a very powerful element in our business development activity.

But is it ethical?

Before anyone begins to think that this is all to do with knavery and trickery we should emphasise one point. None of these tactics are designed to disadvantage the prospective client. Indeed quite the opposite. They are designed to produce a better offer for the prospect. We have no time for tricks and cons pulled at a client's expense. Not only do we take an ethical position on this issue, we also believe that in the long run it is bad for business. When tactics are employed at the client's expense the client is almost certain to find out at some point that she has been taken advantage of or duped. And that is the end of the relationship.

Bearing in mind all of the above we *are* definitely attempting to disadvantage our competitors.

IMPLEMENTING THE LANCHESTER CONCENTRATED ATTACK

We do not know what activities preceded our HR Consultant's initial meeting with his prospective client. This meeting may have been part of a Lanchester approach and the meeting therefore represented an important part of Stage 7 – On the Ground Spying (see Chapter 2).

If this was so then the HR Consultant was taking a risk in the first face-to-face meeting with his Defined Prospect. To have such a discussion and to only field one person is a situation that should be avoided. The HR Consultant should have taken along a colleague of a similar position and stature to himself. If the chemistry between one person and the prospective client is not good initially, then there is an alternative. Also having two people in a meeting means that there are two pairs of ears to pick up any subtle points that one person may miss and after the meeting there are two informed brains that can work out how to try to take the relationship forward. Having two credible people at the meeting also sends out a signal to the prospective client that the firm is serious about wanting to work with her business and has significant, meaningful resource to deploy.

Let us assume that this is a Lanchester approach (solo first meeting mistake aside). On returning to his office the HR Consultant sends a short e-mail to all of his colleagues on the 'task force' team assigned to this Key Defined Prospect. He gives a brief outline of the meeting and the opportunity he has unearthed. He suggests that Stage 8 (Yes / No Decision Point) is a formality. The prospect looks just as good from the inside as the outside and, in the reasonably near future, there is the prospect of profitable work for which the firm is well suited. He advises his colleagues that the prospect is committed to a next step but he would welcome their ideas at a Lanchester team meeting as to how they should be seeking to use the next eight weeks in order to position themselves as favourites for the work.

The ideas that could be generated at that meeting may include things like the following:

- Meet with the Divisional Directors in order to gain an on-the-ground, 'operations' perspective on the need for a new appraisals process. Understand their views and concerns and demonstrate to them that their input will influence the firm's final proposal submission.

- Invite the HR Director (and possibly his colleagues) to any suitable seminars, workshops or round tables that the firm is running over the next few weeks.

- Invite the prospect's team to an appropriate corporate hospitality event. Try to ensure that this is a small scale and reasonably intimate event with possibly a few really well disposed clients also in attendance.

- Encourage the prospective client to take references early. The HR Director said that this would be a critical part of their decision making so don't leave it until the end or be reactive. Invite the client to go along to appropriate businesses where the firm has had similar successes – to see the system in operation and to talk with people with whom the firm has worked.

- Fix a separate meeting with the Director of Training to discuss the potential shape of a train-the-trainer programme. Ensure that the firm takes along a training expert with a proven track record in this sort of work. The training expert should be armed with some examples of previous work carried out for other clients.

- Set up a meeting with the HR Manager to talk further about his idea for a 'how to' manual. Take along a colleague who has experience of writing this type of document and bring examples of previous work that will help to stimulate discussion and clarify the HR Manager's thoughts.

- Having met with the Divisional Directors try to agree a next contact point with them in order to keep dialogue going.

We know that not all of these ideas will work in this particular instance or will be accepted by the prospective client – but they do provide the ammunition for the Stage 9 – Concentrated Attack – phase.

RESPONDING TO TENDERS AND PITCH OPPORTUNITIES (BLUEBIRDS)

Defining Bluebirds

One of the downsides of being well known within a particular professional discipline is that a firm may be asked by all sorts of prospective clients to bid for their work. The post is opened one morning and in it we find an Invitation to Tender or an invitation to pitch the firm's capabilities at a 'beauty parade'. And what is wrong with that, many professionals ask us? In sales parlance these unexpected opportunities are known as 'bluebirds' – pretty creatures that 'fly in through the window'. However, not all feathered creatures are bluebirds. Some are emus – birds that will never fly. Some may be albatrosses – creatures we would not want around our neck.

Three examples of bluebirds

Example 1

On one of our workshops a well known and highly respected lawyer gave us the following anecdote. At a meeting with one of her best clients the client said to her that she needed to be aware that they were going out to tender for their future legal work. "They must have sensed by something in my reaction that this had taken me by surprise", said the lawyer. "I was a little taken aback because the work and the relationship were going ever so well – but I had tried to hide my shock. Having sensed my reaction the client quickly said to me, 'Don't worry, there's no problem. We'll appoint you again but we need to go through this process due to our internal rules. Actually, we were wondering if you could help us to write the tender document?'"

The tender document was duly written and went out to a number of firms who must have concluded that this was a nice bluebird as they spent considerable man days in formulating their written responses. To what end? They never stood a chance of winning the work. They never stood a chance of even being taken seriously.

Example 2

This second example involves the public sector. A property consultant who had spent 18 months on secondment to a very substantial central government department's property section told us this story. He had been party to the appointment of a number of professional advisory firms including engineers, other property advisors and lawyers. Our discussion at the time had been on the subject of procurement processes and in particular the use of Decision Matrices. (A Decision Matrix is a tool that has the names of bidding firms down the left hand column and a number of important Bases of Decision criteria along the top, with certain criteria having different weightings. The aim is to score each bidder on a one to ten scale on each of the criteria. Once the mathematics are worked out then the winner is the firm with the highest score. Nice and objective – and provides an audit trail as to how decisions were made and how firms came to be appointed.)

Looking a little askance the property consultant opined, "I'd be a little careful about taking these decision matrices too seriously. What I observed and what I took part in at (Government Ministry) didn't quite work that way. What tended to happen was that when we knew who we preferred to work with, we scored the decision matrix accordingly!." So much for the even playing field!

He told a specific anecdote about one appointment of lawyers. There was a lot of ongoing work from this ministry so the work concerned was highly prized. The ministry, with a lot of input from the seconded property consultant, created an Invitation to Tender. This was sent out mainly to major London law firms that had a reputation for real estate expertise.

"The firm that came last," said the property consultant, "we never heard from until their written document landed on the mat at the eleventh hour. In addition to the proposal all of the firms also had the chance to do a one hour pitch but they had to field the team who would carry out the work. On the pitch day this team turned up led by a Senior Partner. A seemingly aloof sort of fellow, he introduced his team. They said 'Hello' and then he proceeded to deliver the whole presentation. At the end he fielded every question and his team concluded their contribution by saying 'Goodbye'. It wasn't hard to find the appropriate scores."

"The team that won took a totally different approach. When they received our ITT one of the Partners gave my boss a call. He said that his firm was really keen to win this work but that, as good as the ITT was, there was lots of detail that they would like to bottom out in order to really understand the brief. Could they come in and talk with us? My boss said, 'Yes'. It transpired that one meeting led on to another and then another. The first partner was involved in them all but other lawyers also participated in some meetings. A few of our team got involved in these discussions and we got to know these lawyers. They were nice people. Don't get me wrong, they were good property people but we also felt comfortable with them and whoever the ministry appointed there would be an on-going relationship over at least a two year period. Their proposal was a good one – more in-depth and specific to our needs than most of the others and their pitch again reflected the work they had done up front. Also they made use of all of their whole team in the one hour, most of whom we had already met. It wasn't a difficult decision. We put the appropriate scores on the doors and we chose the people that we liked – again."

Example 3

Contrast example 2 to the experience of a group of lawyers from a well-known London based firm with international capabilities. A partner told us of the following experience.

"We had received a written Invitation to Tender from a German company. They are a global concern and would be a dream client for us. We were told that there would be two significant interactions in the bidding process. The first was a two hour face-to-face briefing meeting at their headquarters in Germany. At this meeting we could ask any questions that we needed in order to construct our pitch. The second was the pitch itself – a couple of weeks later, again at their HQ. Just before the first meeting was due the client cancelled. They said that they didn't have time to see us. They had other priorities but they still wanted us to come along and pitch. We had to put the pitch together based purely on the written document. A team of four of us travelled from London to Germany to make the pitch. It didn't go well right from the outset. You could see from their body language that they were not really interested. In hindsight we believe that we were just there to be ticked off the list – in case anyone in the future asked, 'Did you ask (international law firm) to bid for this?'. We are a very credible name but it was clear that these people did not want us."

At the end of his explanation the lawyer asked us, "What would you have done, given this situation?" Our reply – "We would have 'no bid' the opportunity. We wouldn't have touched it. Once the briefing meeting was cancelled we would have gone back to the prospect thanking them for considering us but then giving a cogent reason why on this occasion we thought it inappropriate to bid."

"We couldn't do that," responded the lawyer, "our Managing Partner would never allow us to not pursue the chance of winning work from (German company)!"

If that were true then the Managing Partner in question has a strange view of business development and an even stranger perspective on profitability. How much did it cost for four Partners to prepare and deliver a presentation in Germany – with zero chance of winning?

To pursue or not to pursue – the bluebird checklist

We are not suggesting that all ITT and beauty parade bluebirds are a waste of time. However, we know that many are. What still continues to surprise us in so many professional firms is the indiscriminate deployment of resources used in chasing bluebirds that will never fly. A question we often ask is, "Of all the opportunities you receive to bid for work, what percentage do you take up?" To this day this question can be met with puzzled looks and responses like, "What do you mean by percentage? We pursue them all." As if any other course of action was somehow illogical! How can these same firms claim that they do not have enough resource to dedicate toward those more effective marketing and business development activities that remain stuck on their wish list?

If any firm believes that these messages about ITTs and beauty parades are an irrelevance to them and that they buck the trend, we don't have a problem with their position. We would only ask that they confirm this belief to themselves by examining their five proposal conversion rates that we outlined earlier in this chapter. However, if a firm recognises these issues – and they are of some concern – then one action that should be taken is the construction of a Bluebird Checklist.

The checklist, an example of which is shown on the next page, enables a professional or business unit head to more objectively review an unexpected opportunity that 'flies in the window'. Often the answers to the questions may be in the 'Query' column. That should be the signal to pick up the telephone and speak with the prospective client or others who may be able to give insight into the answers to these questions. If enough ticks end up in the 'Unfavourable' column then the decision should be made not to engage in pursuit of the work apparently on offer.

Example of a Bluebird Checklist

Name: _____ Date: _____

Bluebird name: _____

	Favourable	Unfavourable	Query
Is the prospect in a targeted industry sector?	Yes	No	Don't know
Is the prospect financially resilient?	Yes	No	Don't know
Is probity an issue?	No	Yes	Don't know
Is there any possibility of conflict of interest with existing clients?	No	Yes	Don't know
Has the opportunity arisen as a result of good personal contacts within the prospect? Do those contacts see this as a real opportunity?	Yes	No	Don't know
Is the client likely to be fee sensitive?	No	Yes	Don't know
Is the work likely to provide our minimum profitability or better?	Yes		Don't know
Do we have the resources to pursue and successfully deliver this opportunity?	Likely	Unlikely	Don't know
Is the location of the client desirable?	Yes	No	Don't know
Is the value of the immediate business worth more than £x,000	Yes	No	Don't know
Is there a prospect of substantial follow-up business?	Yes	No	Don't know
Are less than four other competitors bidding?	Yes	No	Don't know
Is the volume of work to get to proposal stage of a reasonable level?	Yes	No	Don't know
Does the prospect have an identifiable and autonomous Decision Making Process (DMP)?	Yes	No	Don't know
Does the prospect have a reputation as a 'time waster'?	No	Yes	Don't know
Is this prospect a big spender on our type of advice?	Yes	No	Don't know

Action taken: _____

On one workshop that we ran, the Managing Director took away the action point to construct his business's Bluebird Checklist. He produced the finished article at a follow up workshop a few weeks later. Initial impressions were that it looked somewhat similar to the example on the previous page. He introduced his work as follows. "You will notice that the first check item is, 'Did we know about this piece of work before we received the tender document or Request for Proposal (RFP)?' The second reads, 'Can we gain access to talk with the client about this opportunity?' Then you will notice a heavy line. The way it works is that if you get a 'No' answer to the first two questions, then don't bother looking at any of the other factors. You will be wasting your time. I have looked back over the last two years and all of the bluebirds that we have bid for. I have to tell you that I cannot find one instance when we have had a 'No' to both of these two questions, where we have ever won the work."

Our own personal experiences (as illustrated in example 1) of having been given clear indications by clients that work is ours and is 'in the bag' before a proposal has ever been submitted by any bidder, must suggest that this happens to others – including our competitors. If this is so then there must be occasions when the pitch has been tilted so far against us that to bid for some work represents poor use of the firm's resources and our own time.

It is time to be realistic, not optimistic.

MANAGING THE PROJECTING PHASE PROCESS

A few years ago when talking with a group of IT consultants on the subject of sales forecasting one of the group said something like: "It seems that those bids where you rate your chances really highly are the ones that you lose and those where you think that you have no chance you end up winning. I can't see the point in trying to forecast!"

It perhaps comes as no surprise to learn that as we explored further we found that the consultants in question had little understanding of what constituted a successful and replicable selling process. Moreover they had never considered the issue that their potential clients went through a buying process – however unplanned and unstructured it may have been. No wonder they had no idea as to which bids they were likely to win. Their forecasting, such as it was, was based on guesswork.

The fact is that people who are consistently successful in selling their services and the services of their firm, do have a replicable process. Selling is not a black art or something to do only with personality. Professionals who discipline themselves to apply the processes covered in this chapter will win in competitive situations more often. It is that simple.

WHERE TO GO FROM HERE

Where to go from here if you run a firm or have overall responsibility for marketing and business development

Ensure that all practice areas and market facing groups within the firm are measuring their proposal success rate in the five different selling scenarios. Examine this information, conclude what it is telling you and then put in place an action plan to capitalise on strengths and address weaknesses.

Ensure that each practice area or market facing group in the firm has a relevant Bluebird Checklist and that this tool is being used to assess unexpected opportunities.

If you have reason to believe that the selling process (and selling skills) of your professionals are not strong, then invest in appropriate training. The best salespeople in the commercial world took years to hone their selling skills and probably attended weeks of relevant training programmes. Don't be fooled into thinking that because professionals are clever that they can learn these same skills in an afternoon. Any skill takes time to learn, practise and embed.

Where to go from here if you run a business unit within a professional firm

Go along to selling meetings with professionals in your business unit to see for yourself the process and skills that your people employ in these types of meetings. Offer coaching and training to your people if your observations indicate that there is room for improvement.

Before you endorse any individual or group within your team to become engaged in hours or days of proposal production, insist that you want to know the answers to the commercial qualification questions.

In your practice area devise your own tailored Bluebird Checklist and use this to examine all incoming, unexpected opportunities.

Within your practice area measure your professionals' proposal success rate in the five different selling scenarios. Examine this information, conclude what it is telling you and then put in place an action plan to capitalise on strengths and address weaknesses.

Where to go from here if you are a marketing or business development professional working with fee-earners

Get involved in selling meetings with the professionals with whom you work. Try to attend such meetings as an observer, not as a participant. This will help you to focus more clearly and objectively on the meeting dynamics. Provide coaching and feedback to the professionals concerned based on what you have seen and heard.

Encourage the professionals with whom you work to spend a few minutes with you prior to their selling meetings to talk through how they are intending to structure and handle the meeting and the objectives they are seeking to achieve. Coach and give input that will help them to be better prepared and organised.

Work alongside your professionals to help them configure the best way to take forward the selling opportunities they are presented with. Ensure that there is not a default action of rushing to the proposal stage.

Push back when you are presented with poorly qualified selling opportunities and weak bluebirds where you are expected to contribute to the proposal compilation. Your role is to help the firm win business, not to engage in fruitless activity.

Where to go from here if you are an individual practitioner within a professional firm

Adopt the PACES process for your selling meetings. It will give you a framework to work with.

When in future you identify an opportunity for work in either a client or prospective client situation, make it a habit to commercially qualify the business. This practice alone could save you hundreds of hours and help you focus on the really winnable opportunities.

On the next occasion when you are pursuing a very attractive piece of work in a competitive situation, make a specific effort to work out ways that you could move the goalposts and wrong foot your competitors.

When a suitable situation arises next, try a Trojan Horse approach. Practise articulating exactly how you will present it to your client before you meet.

Chapter 5   **Cross-selling**

The titles of the three previous chapters of this book have mirrored the first three segments of The PACE Pipeline – Prospecting, Promoting and Projecting. The next chapter is called Pruning. It would seem logical that this chapter is entitled Protecting. However, protecting client relationships is a far larger subject than just being able to sell and market to them successfully. Indeed it is such a large (and important) subject to professional services firms that we have devoted a whole book, *Managing Key Clients* to the topic. Because this book is dedicated to the subject of managing business development, this chapter is focused upon one element of client management – the issue of how to sell more of a firm's services in an existing relationship – cross-selling.

Before proceeding we should define exactly what we mean by cross-selling. Our definition is as follows:

Gaining the client's willing acceptance to meet with professionals from other disciplines, offices or practice areas that have not previously carried out work with this client. The purpose of the dialogue is to explore the opportunities for adding value to the client relationship through the provision of additional areas of our expertise.

We are not talking about a property valuation expert returning from a client meeting and saying to a property management professional, "I've just won some work for you. I've got the instructions in my briefcase!" These things don't happen and on the rare occasions that they do, they create problems not plaudits. What sort of work would someone with his expertise in valuations win for a professional in property management? What impossible agreements might this person have made in all good faith? What fee rates would have been quoted and what would these rates include?

Professionals have to negotiate their own business. Cross-selling is all about providing a colleague with a warm environment with an existing client in which to seek out and win new work.

Few firms have achieved real success in consistently being able to cross-sell their capabilities. As one Managing Partner once said to us, "If we could cross-sell more effectively we could hit our fee income objectives for the next five years and never have to win one new client. I keep on at my people about this. It seems such a logical route but apart from occasional successes we are not really making much progress. Do other firms have this problem?"

Well, if misery loves company, then this Managing Partner has lots of counterparts to be miserable with. We refer to success in cross-selling as the Holy Grail. All firms are seeking it and it is a very elusive object.

For something that is just so logical to be such a rare occurrence would suggest that there are some very real barriers to implementation. Over the last eight years we have studied the issue of cross-selling. We have discussed the subject with dozens of firms and hundreds, if not thousands, of individual professionals. We have concluded that there are definite and specific barriers within firms that militate against success in this activity.

We have identified eight separate barriers and have created a 'healthcheck' tool whereby professionals within a firm can assess which of the barriers, in their opinion, have the greatest impact upon the firm's ability to cross-sell its services.

The steps firms need to take in order to release the potential fee-income and profitability that could be unlocked through successful cross-selling, are simple. Firstly they need to agree, honestly and objectively, which of the barriers apply to their business. Secondly they need to put in place the actions that will reduce the effect of these barriers. In this chapter we will examine each of the eight barriers and suggest what firms can do about them.

There could be nine barriers but we have already explored the ninth in some depth in our book *Creating New Clients*. The ninth is this. If the client does not regard the professional who is attempting to cross-sell to her as a trusted advisor then the attempt will almost always be unsuccessful. When examining the eight remaining barriers we will work on the assumption that the person who manages the relationship with the client (and who is therefore the person who has the opportunity to cross-sell) is considered by the client to be a trusted advisor.

THE BARRIERS AND HOW TO REDUCE THEIR EFFECT

Communication

One of the most common symptoms of a firm that is failing to make the best of the cross-selling opportunities that must inevitably arise in day to day dialogue with clients, is the existence of what is referred to as 'silo mentality'.

Silo mentality starts because people whose work involves spending nearly all of their time with the same set of people (e.g. the people in their department or the people on their floor) see little reason to communicate with the wider organisation. At the outset there is no malicious intent in this behaviour. Generally the individuals are working hard but solely focused on their own objectives and roles.

However, any department, practice area or office that becomes so insular that it fails to communicate well with the rest of the organisation is highly unlikely to cross-sell others' capabilities. Likewise they are not likely to benefit from others cross-selling their abilities and services.

Silo mentality not only has an effect on a business's ability to cross-sell. It will always have other negative impacts. When silo mentality hardens, people lose sight of how their work and behaviour impacts upon others. Teamworking inevitably suffers. A blame culture can also develop. When things go wrong (as they invariably do in an environment where poor communication and teamworking prevail) departments are more concerned to prove that they are without guilt in respect of problems that arise. Therefore the guilt – and the blame – lie elsewhere.

Whilst silo mentality, poor communication and poor teamworking are rarely consciously initiated, these behaviours can quickly contribute to a very corrosive way of operating.

To reduce the cross-selling barrier caused by poor communication:

- Avoid (wherever possible) locating people in numerous buildings and on many floors.

- Create a physical working environment that encourages people to talk to each other. (Get rid of unnecessary physical barriers.)

- Create common areas where people from different parts of the firm can get together. (We have been told on more than one occasion that the best connected and informed people within a firm are the firm's smokers!)

- Create a lunching area – and make a real effort to ensure that this area becomes habitual for most people taking a longer break from their working day. Discourage people from eating at their desks or in their departments.

- Organise primarily by market (or client) facing teams rather than by practice area or by department. This will usually result in virtual multi-disciplinary teams forming, carrying out work and then disbanding on a regular basis.

- Organise events, whether business or social, where people from all over the firm attend. For instance, in some forms of training mixed groups are perfectly acceptable. 'Stage manage' such events in order that people cannot circulate purely within their own clique.

- Insist that Partners and other influential individuals within the firm be seen to be role models of good communication with others outside their immediate interest area.

Knowledge of what others do

It has long been recognised that business developers need strong 'product' knowledge in order to be successful. One cannot sell to a discerning buyer if one's product knowledge is at an insufficient level. There is no suggestion that a professional must know everything about every capability of every practice area and every office within the firm. This would be an impossible quest. However, a professional who is willing to engage in cross-selling must know enough about other capabilities of his firm in order to persuade the client to engage in dialogue with one of his colleagues.

Lack of knowledge can exist on two levels. These are:
- An absolute lack of knowledge.
- A lack of accurate and up-to-date information.

Absolute lack of knowledge is prevalent in very large firms – but can be found on occasions in much smaller professional practices as well. There have been countless times when we have worked with mixed skills groups in major firms where people have admitted to the person sitting next to them, "You know, I didn't even know that we had the capability to do what you do. How long have you worked for the firm?"

Given this situation it is hardly surprising that these 'new' people get very few introductions into the firm's existing client base and are often reduced to prospecting for new client work.

A lack of accurate and up-to-date information pervades most firms. The Banking team may know the headlines of what the Corporate team does but they probably have little idea of the latest capabilities of the Corporate team. Additionally, they would have difficulty in articulating, in an effective and convincing manner, the capabilities of which they are aware.

Whilst the archetypal salesman may try baffling the customer in order to hide his lack of product knowledge, most professionals quite rightly recoil from this type of behaviour. People who are paid to be right have no desire to be put in situations where they can be 'caught out'.

The suggestion from a professional that, "You should talk with one of my colleagues in X Department; I believe that they could assist you", is likely to be followed by some questions from the client. Few professionals are going to make such a suggestion to a client unless they feel reasonably equipped to deal with ensuing questions – without being 'caught out'.

To reduce the cross-selling barrier caused by a lack of knowledge of what others do:

- Insist that a core element of the firm's Continuous Professional Development (CPD) consists of staying abreast of the capabilities that the firm has to offer its client base. There should be a demand from the top of the firm for people to continue to learn.

- Ensure that practice group leaders put aside some time on a regular basis in order to meet with their colleagues from other parts of the firm with a view to educating them on the department's latest products and services. (30 minute informal lunchtime meetings could be considered as a vehicle.)

- Where possible arrange for secondments to other practice areas – with secondees charged with the responsibility of educating their colleagues upon return to their own department.

- Invest in an intranet site that allows professionals to find for themselves most of the information about another practice area's capabilities and people – if there is no one to ask.

- Insist that each practice area is responsible for keeping its intranet information up to date in order that others in the firm can rely on its contents.

- Consider investing in an 'intelligent' knowledge management software solution that provides information on any aspect of the firm's operations.

Trust in others' capabilities

As individuals we would never buy important services from someone we felt we could not trust. Therefore it is highly unlikely that we will recommend to others the services of those in whom we do not have absolute faith. Our reluctance will be even greater if we believe that such an introduction will one day backfire badly as the client realises who it was that made the original recommendation.

Unless professionals are trusted implicitly they will never be on the receiving end of cross-selling opportunities from their peers.

Lack of trust can develop in two main ways.

Situation 1. In this instance we may have evidence that a fellow professional is technically weak or is insufficiently skilled in dealing with certain situations or types of client. (Unfortunately there are occasions when this lack of ability or skill pervades entire practice areas or whole offices – usually due to a lack of enforced high standards.)

The case for lack of trust in others' abilities is reinforced where there are specific, documented examples of client work that have been badly managed or delivered by another department. If the business in question was won as a result of a cross-selling effort, then the situation is even worse.

Situation 2. In many instances however, the 'evidence' of poor performance or lack of client orientation is weak, unproven and exaggerated by rumour. Add to this a lack of understanding as to the capabilities of the 'offender' plus an unwillingness to communicate on a potentially very sensitive subject. Result? There is a *belief* that the other party is incapable and therefore not to be trusted with a valued client.

When it comes to whom we trust, belief is every bit as important as facts.

To reduce the barriers caused by a lack of trust in others' capabilities:

- Insist on high standards of management and delivery of all work to all clients – irrespective of the source of the work.

- Provide all support and training necessary to underperformers in order that they have the opportunity to develop quickly to the firm's required standards.

- Don't be tempted to keep people or practice areas that are not operating to a high standard – even if they are providing useful fee income and profitability today. This sends out the wrong message and the profitability will only be temporary in any case.

- Get rid of people or practice areas that cannot (in spite of encouragement and adequate training) consistently manage and deliver client work to the required standards.

- Sack people who see referred work as 'for free' – and therefore have less commitment to deliver this type of work to the highest standards.

- Don't allow cross-sold introductions to be 'thrown over the fence' or 'dragged over the fence'. Ensure that the cross-seller makes an effective introduction of his colleague – attending at least the first meeting between his colleague and the client.

- Insist that the introduced professional keeps the cross-seller informed of all developments with the client.

- Where there are poor relationships between parts of the firms that should be cross-referring work, bring them together. Insist that they talk openly and honestly about the real (and perceived) issues that cause them to avoid cross-referring.

Use a professional facilitator to run such interventions. If it were to be poorly managed this type of encounter could result in entrenched positions and attitudes.

- Refer to the suggestions under the previous subject heading of Communication. Very often Lack of Trust problems and Communication problems are intertwined.

Loss of control considerations

Probably the greatest barrier to cross-selling in a firm is a high level of insecurity felt by professional staff. Feelings of insecurity affect the behaviour of people in many negative ways.

For example 'owning' the relationship with a highly prized and valuable client is one way in which an individual can compensate. Knowing that the firm relies on the professional for access to the client creates a feeling of power – critical in an environment where insecurity prevails. Some professionals, who have worked in a number of firms that have this aura of insecurity, have built their careers on moving from firm to firm - taking their key clients with them. It is clear that the relationship is with the individual and not with the firm for which they work. Such people are almost never willing to introduce other colleagues into 'their' clients, as this would diminish the total ownership that they hold over the relationship.

Professionals who feel insecure are also unwilling to introduce clients to their colleagues because they fear that once their colleagues begin a relationship with the client, they will not know everything that is going on within the client. Their feelings of security are tied into the certainty of being in control – and giving another person licence to 'do their thing' with your client is a sure way to weaken that certainty.

This feeling is exacerbated when the professional believes that some of his/her colleagues could be threatening because of their high capability. The last thing that an insecure person needs is to be negatively benchmarked by the client against a colleague who is perceived to be brighter, more knowledgeable, more personable or more client orientated.

On the face of it, this very major barrier to effective cross-selling lies deep within individuals. This is only partially true. The question must be asked, "Why do these individuals behave in this way – or, more significantly, why is this behaviour endemic in some firms?"

Where this behaviour is common and widespread within a firm it is because the firm supports and fosters a culture of fear. Professionals quickly realise that the path to security and success is to grab any opportunity that arises and never to share the spoils with others. An opportunity shared is recognition halved, could well be the motto.

Whilst many people find such a working atmosphere abhorrent, the fighters and scrappers, the strong and the politically adept thrive in such a challenging environment. New day, new battles to be won.

We find that these problems invariably start at the top of the organisation. The whole firm is usually a mirror of the behaviours of those who run it.

Alternatively the firm may have weak management. Management recognises the 'my client' issue. They can identify the people who are the acidic role models. However they are unwilling to take actions that will change the prevailing behaviour. This is often because these negative role model figures are recognised – using current metrics - as the most successful and productive in the firm. To challenge their behaviour would be to run the risk of losing them – and the client relationships that they control.

Those firms that actively seek to recruit lateral hires who bring significant client relationships with them, run the risk of importing this insular, self focused way of thinking and behaving. However, the short term gain of additional fee income for the firm is usually too much of a temptation to resist.

To reduce the cross-selling barrier caused by loss of control considerations takes time and strong management:

- Firstly the senior people within the firm must act as positive role models. They must be seen to be active in bringing colleagues from other parts of the business into their client relationships.

- Senior management must identify what causes the aura of fear within their business – and they must tackle this and eliminate it. This may mean changing their own behaviour quite substantially.

- The metrics for measuring success must be changed. Professionals solely measured (and rewarded) on chargeable hours carried out by themselves – or their department – have no reason to cross-sell others' capabilities, or indeed carry out any activity that is for the long term good health of the firm.

- The negative role models have to be 'worked out' of the firm – even though this will probably have a short term financial impact. Whilst these individuals are allowed to flourish and set the cultural tone, no-one will believe the stated commitment of management to build a culture where sharing and supporting one another is a demonstrable core value.

An example related to points two and three above arose during a series of research meetings with a number of professionals who worked for a property consultancy. One particular individual had been very successful in building up a practice area from scratch and it was obvious that he had enjoyed the process. His talent was rare in the firm. It had many doers but few genuine business developers. It was clear that he had an identifiable, replicable model for doing what he had achieved. However, his success meant that he was now stretched in carrying out the work he had generated.

When asked the question, "Why, instead of doing the work, don't you continue to build the business for others, selling their capability?" his answer was as follows.
"To create the time to do this I would have to give a lot of my current clients - and the work they generate - to others. If it should happen that the market changed quickly I could be left with very little fee-earning work. That's all that is measured in this firm. In such a situation I know that I would be amongst the first who would be asked to go. The track record of this firm is that if you don't have a desk full of work you'll be made redundant when times get tough."

Fear kills people's motivation to cross-sell and fear can be either generated by, or implicitly supported by, senior management. Exhortations by these same senior figures for professionals to cross-sell their colleagues' capabilities fall on deaf ears.

Financial considerations

Why should any individual dedicate effort, time and resource to cross-sell his colleagues' services when the very success of the endeavour will have a negative financial effect on his practice area or on him personally? We have heard it said; "If you ask me to do 'x' and pay me to do 'y', then what do you think I will do?" Senior management repeating the mantra of everyone 'doing what is best for the firm' cuts little ice if the individual who is asked to do the doing, suffers in the process. Helping others should not be at the expense of the helpers.

In poorly disciplined firms some work generated from clients may be carried out by an office in the wrong geographical location or without the resources to deliver the work to the standards that could be delivered by other practice areas. In reality a different office or practice group would better serve the client. It would therefore be in the best interests of the firm and the client if others' capabilities were cross-sold.

However the incumbents are usually loath to surrender their client as they recognise that their fee income will be reduced and, as a consequence, the earnings of those currently engaged on the client's work may also suffer.

Geographical differences can also affect cross-selling in another way. The fees charged by one office may be much less (or more) than those charged by another. A client who is cross-sold the services of a low fee-rate office (or practice area) may demand that all future fees be at the lower level. This clearly makes high fee-rate offices nervous about introducing their colleagues from lower fee-rate offices. Even worse than their own fee rates coming under pressure is the fear that the client may play cute – and ask that all future work is managed from the lower fee office.

In some circumstances clients may have a budget for how much they can spend on certain professional services. Cross-selling a colleague to these clients means yet another competitor for the (limited) budget.

In some firms none of the above examples of Financial Considerations apply. However, whilst there may be no negative financial impacts related to cross-selling others' services, likewise there are no financial incentives. Few people work purely for money but money is a very tangible way of rewarding those behaviours that the firm is trying to encourage.

To reduce the cross-selling barrier caused by financial considerations:

- Understand *from the fee-earners' perspective* what they see as the negative Financial Considerations related to cross-selling others' services.

- Act to defuse these as appropriate.

- Set rules and guidelines on who can sell (and service) different skill sets in different markets and geographical sectors. Do not allow cross border banditry driven by financial reward – or greed!

- Enforce the rules - and be prepared to move clients from their current relationship manager if it can be demonstrated that the client work is being carried out purely for financial motives whilst putting at risk either:
    The quality of the client work or client relationship management.
    The quality of the relationship with the firm.
    The internal harmony of the business.

- Over time, drive out of the system all of the old anomalies of client 'ownership' motivated for financial reasons.

- Be tough on offices and practice areas that are seen to try to steal work and clients from others. Don't allow it to happen.

- Give real rewards for cross-selling – including financial rewards.

- Be innovative and break the accepted ways of recognising and rewarding people. One firm that has fewer problems than most when it comes to cross-selling its services allows both the giver and the receiver to claim credit for the business won. They double count – and double reward – and have no client ownership problems motivated by Financial Considerations. Conversely in other firms the leaders just purse their lips, knowing this could never be done for a host of 'rational' reasons. Their firms then still face this Financial Considerations barrier with no positive motivation in place for their fee-earners to cross-sell.

Knowing how to cross-sell

Most professionals are unaware that they don't know how to cross-sell. The reason is that they don't know what they don't know.

When professionals tell us that they have attempted to cross-sell the capabilities of one of their colleagues but have received a polite turndown (and existing clients are always likely to be polite and courteous when they reject an offer from an incumbent trusted advisor) we ask them to talk us through exactly what happened. It is not unusual to hear something that goes like the following.

"Well, we had been talking and on a couple of occasions the client made reference to a new transaction that was on the horizon. Now I know that we do that sort of work and I know the people who do it. They're very good and I would have no hesitation in recommending them, so that's what I did. I said to the client, 'Do you know, you should speak with my colleagues in our XYZ Department. They do this work all the time. They are extremely good and I would recommend that you speak with them. I can arrange for John Smith the lead partner to give you a call.' The client made some comment about already having a short list of people that they would consider for the work so, 'Thank you for the offer and if the situation changes we'll get back to you'. But that's wishful thinking. She meant 'No' in the nicest possible way. I didn't want to push it. That would only have strained my relationship. But no one can say that I didn't try."

Try, yes – but in a completely firm-centric manner. Think about it from the client's point of view. What's in it for the client? Where's the added value? In the instance above, instead of considering (perhaps) three options, now the client has to consider four – and the fourth option will probably demand more of the client's time in order to generate a realistic proposal as the two parties have not worked together before. Not exactly a compelling proposition from the client's perspective is it?

Before attempting to cross-sell the professional must have thought through the proposition from the client's perspective. He must then *be able to articulate* why it would be good for the client to engage in discussions with other people from his firm - over and above any other competitors that client may either be dealing with today or considering in the future.

The argument must be client-centric. The simple question is, "Where is the benefit for the client?"

Similar scenarios occur every day in firms when one professional wishes to be introduced to a client whose relationship is managed by an incumbent partner. Rarely does the supplicant ever spend any time thinking through how his proposition to sell his services is going to assist the current client partner. The mindset is, "This is going to help me." At best it could be, "This is for the good of the firm." Seeing no benefits for him and his team the incumbent partner therefore resists the approach by insisting that: "It is not the right time" and that, "The client is engaged in other issues right now."

To reduce the barriers caused by not knowing how to cross-sell:

- Educate professionals in order that they have explicit understanding of the difference between a client-focused attempt to cross-sell and a firm-focused attempt.

- Provide training for professionals who are expected to cross-sell. Highly developed listening skills are the single most important attribute of a consistently successful business developer. Ensure that the training has sufficient focus on this skill.

- Make sure that during the training participants have time to practise and practise again how they approach cross-selling opportunities. Like any skill, real expertise is built upon practice - not upon having an intellectual grasp of the concept.

- Before any prepared attempt to cross-sell is carried out, insist on a 'rehearsal' when feedback and suggestions can be given. Ten minutes invested the day prior can often mean the difference between success and failure.

A real understanding of the client's business

Like some marriages, business relationships between client and advisor can settle down to be comfortable but undemanding. The initial exploration by both sides at the beginning of the relationship practically ceases and, particularly if there is a good flow of profitable work for the professional, his time is mainly taken up executing this work. The professional becomes expert in this particular (often very limited) part of the client's business and becomes familiar with a (usually small) group of client people who have a direct interest in the work carried out.

Given this scenario – reached after months or years of working with the client – now ask the professional to suggest to the client other ways in which his firm could assist their business, outside of the work in which the firm is engaged today.

The professional 'suddenly' realises how little he knows about the totality of the client's business. This makes cross-selling difficult. In the professional's mind's eye is a picture of his cross-selling attempt being greeted by a raised eyebrow and a surprised, askance look on the client's face. The professional imagines that behind the facial expression the client is thinking: "What a strange thing to suggest. Why would we ever want to pursue that avenue? Doesn't he know how our business works?

Doesn't he know our policy? He has always seemed quite credible up to now but to put that idea forward makes me question my judgement. He's out of his depth and he doesn't really understand our business."

Most professionals only want to suggest ideas that make sense and which their clients would view as potentially valuable, workable and in line with the client's future direction. However, in order to be able to do this the professional needs to have an up to date understanding of:

- The key issues for this client in their marketplace.

- The main 'environmental' (non market related) issues that the client's business is having to face.

- The Critical Success Factors for the client's business that they have to focus upon.

- Given all of these factors, the client's burning issues and priorities.

- The client's business objectives and the strategies they are implementing in pursuit of these objectives.

- The professional advice the client needs as an integral part of the pursuit of their strategy.

- Their policy with regard to sourcing this advice from their current advisors.

- Who, in the client's business, would be involved in making the decisions about the appointment of advisors for this type of work.

Unless a professional has a reasonable handle on the answers to these sorts of questions it is very easy to 'put your foot in it'. A well meaning attempt to cross-sell another part of the firm's capability can be viewed as gauche and 'out of character'.

Fortunately (or perhaps unfortunately) most professionals are clever enough to realise this before they open their mouths. When they catch a glimpse of (what they believe may be) a potential cross-selling opportunity they work on the premise that: "If I keep my mouth closed and say nothing you may think that I am a fool – but if I open my mouth and speak, I will prove that I am."

No-one but the super-confident tries to cross-sell other services unless they are certain of the context surrounding the potential application of these services.

To reduce the barriers caused by a lack of real understanding of the client's business:

- Insist that in every 'business as usual' meeting that a professional takes with a client, that some time – even just five minutes – is spent on stepping back from the immediate priorities to understand what is happening in the client's 'big picture'.

- Invite clients to talk to fee-earners. Ask them to tell you what is going on in their business and in their universe. This not only helps professionals to really understand a client's business, it also demonstrates to clients that the firm is really interested in them and their business situation. Make this a regular event and insist that professionals attend.

- Ensure that in each of the market sectors in which the firm's key clients operate that someone participates in the major client industry conferences and meetings. This will ensure early sight of issues likely to affect the most important clients of the firm. Ensure that the people who attend such events summarise the main points and then distribute their summarised conclusions to all interested parties within the firm.

- Ensure that someone gets invited to major conferences run by key clients. Again, insist that the person attending distributes summary notes to all people involved with the client.

- For each client (where cross-selling appears to provide major opportunities) establish a non-chargeable fee-earner time investment budget. This time is to be used for one of two purposes – either building deeper relationships or providing some form of 'added value' to the client. Added value is an overworked term. Value is only added if *the client* says so. If the client has received something over and above a totally professional service - and they really appreciate the additional effort - then added value has been delivered.

- Consider offering key clients a professional on secondment but ensure that the secondee provides regular updates on the client's business.

- If the firm has a research department then make sure that part of their effort is directed toward keeping up to date on developments, trends and latest news in the markets in which the firm's key clients operate. This information needs to be presented in easily accessible format to professionals working with clients in these markets.

- If a client is substantial, ensure that the professionals engaged in today's client work subscribe to the client's main trade publication in order to keep abreast of market events in general and issues impacting on their client in particular.

- Where major clients would seem to present opportunities for cross-selling, bring the people engaged with the client together to discuss what these opportunities could be and how they could be approached. Ensure that there is one person in the meeting who is a 'neutral' who can challenge the client team and prevent mindless 'group think'.

- Every now and again bring new people into the client team. Involve them in direct contact with the client. As they will usually have a natural desire to learn it is OK for them to ask the client the occasional 'dumb' questions that the client partner would die to know the answers to but would be too afraid to ask.

The client's image of our firm

In the previous section entitled *A real understanding of the client's business* we highlighted the problems that can be caused when the professional's understanding of the client's business fails to develop over time. The relationship goes forward; it may even be more firmly rooted, but the real understanding of the entirety of the client's business can diminish as time passes.

This is a two-way street. In much the same way as the professional's understanding of the client's business calcifies, the same is often true of the client's understanding of the professional's firm. Therefore there is a danger that the firm becomes pigeon-holed in the client's mind. Objective reality counts for nothing. The client's perception is reality.

If, due to the type of work we have carried out for a number of months or years, the client perceives us as a planning specialist, then that is what we are. It does not matter that planning work brings in only 10% of our firm's fee income and only represents 25% of our own personal utilisation. From the client's point of view we spend 100% of our time (with them) on planning work.

When we come to cross-sell this gives us a credibility problem with the client. An attempt to cross-sell the services of our colleagues who are employment specialists can be met with a client mindset (if not actual spoken words) of: "Why would I use a firm of planning specialists for employment work?"

There is no referee to whom the client – or the professional - can turn. Mostly clients will back their own judgement – despite the seemingly poor evidence on which that judgement is based.

To reduce the barriers caused by the client's image of our firm:
- In passing, keep telling the client about the varied, new and different activities in which the firm is engaged. This is not an attempt to sell these capabilities but just a way of keeping them on the client's horizon.

- Ensure that current clients are targeted with marketing messages that keep them abreast of the range of capabilities that the firm has to offer. Send newsletters, copies of case studies, invitations to seminars and copies of press releases to clients where there should be (at some point) good opportunities to cross-sell other services and capabilities.

  However every marketing message must be relevant to the individual to whom it is addressed. We are not suggesting 'carpet bombing' clients with irrelevant mailshots, brochures and invitations. The focus should be on quality not quantity. Also it is important to remember that if the effect of the marketing effort directed toward a client is not positive, then equally it is not neutral. It is negative.

- When the firm has developed a new capability or service and has had demonstrable success, promote this widely in the sorts of places where clients are likely to notice.

WHICH BARRIERS AFFECT YOUR BUSINESS?

The suggestion is not that every professional services firm suffers from the effects of all of these eight barriers. However if just two or three are embedded in a firm's way of thinking or acting then this will explain why the seemingly reasonable and logical objective of cross-selling more of the firm's capabilities to more of its clients is not being realised.

WHERE TO GO FROM HERE

Where to go from here if you run a firm or have overall responsibility for marketing and business development

Carry out an analysis of which of the eight barriers to success in cross-selling applies to your firm. The PACE Cross-selling Healthcheck may be a useful tool to use for this exercise. Do not do this analysis on your own. Involve a cross section of people who are prepared to debate the subject. You will almost certainly get more accurate conclusions.

Having identified the priority barriers, look at the suggestions contained throughout this chapter in how to overcome them. Put in place a corrective action plan. Review this plan each quarter to ensure that progress is being made.

Put in place some form of measurement to assess how cross-selling is improving across the firm.

Ensure that you act as a cross-selling role model for others.

Where to go from here if you run a business unit within a professional firm

If you want your part of the firm to be a recipient of in-bound cross-selling introductions, then put together a plan as to how you will market your part of the business to those other parts of your firm that appear to be your most likely sources. Include a short (20 to 30 minute) presentation on your business unit and the benefits that it brings to your current clients. Illustrate your pitch with examples where possible in order to build people's confidence and trust in your team.

Arrange meetings with parts of the firm that are likely to be introducers of opportunities. Your marketing tools and presentation are not much use if they remain in your office.

Ensure that all incoming introductions and cross-sold work are well-handled initially and then executed professionally. Nothing will kill off introductions and work from other departments more quickly than a poor response by your team.

If your business unit has (or contributes to) an intranet site then ensure that it is always accurate and up to date – so that others in the firm know that they can rely on the information that it contains.

If there is a particular part of the firm from where you believe you should be getting introductions but aren't, then arrange a secondment with this part of the organisation. Get one of your good people into this department and offer to take one of theirs in return.

Where to go from here if you are a marketing or business development professional working with fee earners

Talk with the professionals who manage those major clients where there are perceived to be cross-selling opportunities. Work out a detailed programme of *relevant* marketing activities and tools directed toward interested individuals within these businesses. This is to try to ensure that the firm does not become 'pigeon holed'. In order to ensure that the programme is really relevant firstly be certain that you have a very clear view of the clients' issues and needs.

Provide the relevant professionals with updated summaries of key information related to market sectors in which the firm's key clients operate in order to trigger thinking about potential cross-selling opportunities.

Organise training for those professionals who are likely to come across cross-selling opportunities in order that they are practised in articulating the benefits of the introduction from the client's perspective.

Be prepared to provide coaching to professionals who are about to have client meetings where cross-selling opportunities may arise.

Where to go from here if you are an individual practitioner within a professional firm

Work out which people within your firm could most likely be both the recipients and donors of cross-selling opportunities. It is easier to start with situations where there is potential reciprocity.

Work out exactly how these other people and their clients would benefit through your working with some of their client base. Practise articulating your arguments.

Contact these other people with a view to meeting with them to discuss cross-selling reciprocity.

Before you meet with anyone, work out exactly what you can give to them. Be prepared to give first in order to get the reciprocity process started.

When a colleague gives you an introduction always make sure that you keep them continually posted on your actions and progress.

Take time out with your most important clients to spend a few minutes talking with them about their business and where it is going. Cross-selling opportunities may well result from these new insights.

Chapter 6   **Pruning**

When we are running our Managing Business Development workshops for professionals we (seemingly somewhat perversely) cover this subject before we even begin to examine in any detail how to build a strong pipeline of future business. There is a very good reason for our approach. We know that as professionals are absorbing our messages of what they need to do in order to be successful in new business acquisition, they are also thinking, "But where will I find the time to do all of this? The logic is impeccable but available time is the issue. I have to meet my billing targets first and foremost."

The fact is that many professionals spend part of their fee-earning time working for clients they wished they didn't have. Moreover the firm would be better off if it didn't serve these clients. Our message is simple, if somewhat challenging. If you could dump the work that is low level, low recovery, high hassle and causes low morale in your department, would that provide you with time to carry out business development aimed at winning high value, high profit clients? So why don't you do something about it?

GIGO

There is no doubt in our minds that every professional services firm deals with a proportion of clients where the relationship is unsatisfactory and the firm in question would be better off without the burden of these clients. We regularly hear the anecdotes about 'clients from hell'. One reason for this is that most firms have made very little conscious effort to select the clients that they wish to work with. The selection criteria that we described in Chapter 3 are used by only a small number of more enlightened professional businesses. Also, it must be said that if a prospective client totally unmatched to the selection criteria threw itself at even one of these more enlightened firms, then it is unlikely that the firm would choose to turn away this 'free' business.

Contrast this to the example of advertising agency Leo Burnett. In his book, *The Loyalty Effect*, Frederick Reichheld showed that this firm, statistically, was the most productive and profitable in its industry. It also had far and away the highest client loyalty. Reichheld writes, "…Burnett chooses customers with whom it can earn the right to act as partner. In 1994, of the 54 companies that invited the agency to talk about a business relationship, Burnett pursued only 5. Of its 33 current clients, 12 have been with the firm at least twenty years, 10 for more than thirty years."

Five out of 54! Now that is selection criteria in action. There is no doubt that the GIGO principle has relevance to this subject. An old IT terminology, GIGO is short for Garbage In, Garbage Out.

In other words if a firm starts its business development activity with poor quality prospects then it will result in a client base that contains many poor quality clients. We know of no firm that makes a conscious effort to deliberately pursue unsuitable prospects. However, by failing to use (and stick by) its selection criteria a firm will be building a partially unsuitable client base by default.

In addition, as we pointed out in Chapters 1, 2 (Lanchester Strategy) and 4, a firm should take a raincheck shortly after it has met with a prospective client the first time. Is this really the sort of client that we want to work with? Is this really the sort of work that we want to pursue? The time to answer these questions is early – before the business development process has gained a momentum of its own and everyone is committed to winning the work regardless of the consequences.

Discussing this subject with a team of consulting engineers one of the group said to us, "We have a name for that. We call it the 'Hooray! Damn! Syndrome'." Seeing our look of incomprehension the engineer went on to explain. "We get these situations where we are committed to bidding for a project. You meet with the prospective client quite a lot as you're putting together the proposal. As you do so you realise what an awful, difficult job this is going to be and what dreadful people they are going to be to work with over what could be a very long period of time. But you and your team are just so committed to beating the competition. Then one day after your final pitch you get that call that says you've won the contract. That's when we jump in the air and shout 'Hooray', then stop and say 'Oh damn, how are we ever going to do this?!'" His colleagues laughed, recognising only too well the scenario that their compatriot had described.

The expression, "Our clients will become better when we do", has more than a grain of truth. We should accept that we have the clients that we deserve. No one forced any firm to have the client base it now possesses.

A PRUNING CASE STUDY

This subject always brings to mind a meeting that we had a few years back with the Managing Director of a medium sized consulting engineering business. At one point in the discussion he referred to, "having sacked our biggest client." We had to explore this story further and so we asked him to elaborate.

He explained that the firm's largest client two years previously was responsible for 15% of the firm's total fee income. At the time the client had been a FTSE 100 business. However, the client was a 'problem child'. The problem was the totally arrogant manner of the engineering and maintenance management team of this business. Despite bringing some very specialist engineering skills to the client, the people working for the consultancy were treated like contract labourers.

They were ordered about like lackeys and their expert opinions were very often dismissed. They would arrive early on site for meetings only to find that the client's people had not bothered to turn up. When things went wrong because the client had not carried out their part of the work it was always the consultants who got the blame. Work very often had to be repeated through no fault of the consultants and bills, whilst paid eventually, were haggled over for ages resulting in poor cash flow.

The result was that no one in the firm wanted to carry out work for the client. To be sent on a project with this client was regarded as a sentence. Sickness and absenteeism soared on this client's projects and the firm knew that it had lost good people who had decided to leave rather than face another project with 'the client from hell'. Attempts had been made over the years to try to get some resolution to the issues that constantly arose but nothing had worked. At one board meeting when the troubles caused by this client arose yet again in discussion the Managing Director said, "Perhaps we'd be better off if we sacked this client." This thought was met with immediate knee-jerk rejection. 15% of the fee income disappearing out the door was the thought that quickly sprang to mind. Mulling a little more on the suggestion someone had then asked, "So who would do this?" The MD replied that it was probably his job.

Subsequently a meeting was arranged between the Managing Director and some of the senior management team from the client. The MD approached the meeting with a resolve to present honestly and openly the issues that constantly dogged the projects with this client and, in conjunction with the client's people, to find resolution. He also had an equally clear resolve that if genuine progress could not be made then he would walk away.

After a while it became clear that no real progress was being made. The client's management was there to give orders and the job of the consultants was to listen and obey. That's the way it worked. Having realised that he was getting nowhere he turned to the clients and said, "I'd like to thank you for the work that you have given us over the years. We've got a number of projects that we are working on at the moment that will all be completed over the next few months. We will carry out this work to the highest possible standards as we have always tried to do in the past. However we will not be seeking any more work from your organisation. Thank you." And with that he took his firm's very specialist skills away from the client.

The impact on the professional staff was immediate and powerful. People praised the courageous stance. Morale soared. Sickness, absenteeism and staff turnover reduced. Productivity increased and everyone was committed to finding replacement work. Within 18 months the hole in the fee income stream had been replaced. The MD explained to us that, "This was the best decision we ever made at this firm."

'LACK OF FIT' CRITERIA

There can be a number of reasons why a client does not fit with a firm's minimum standards in order to rate as a valued client. These include the following:

1   The work that the client provides is of low volume or produces low fee income.

2   The work is unprofitable or does not meet absolutely minimum gross profit parameters.

3   The billing process in place or the client's slowness in settling invoices produces poor cash flow.

4   The type of client or the work they generate does not fit with the strategic direction of the firm.

5   Association with the client or the work we carry out for them creates a poor image for our firm in the rest of the marketplace.

6   The client – or the work they provide for us – is unpleasant to deal with.

7   Association with the client or the work they provide leads to low staff morale and / or high staff turnover.

8   The work has a high 'hassle factor' or is a source of constant remedial actions.

9   The work the client provides is not in line with our current / future strengths.

'Problem children' clients most often demonstrate more than one of the above criteria.

IDENTIFYING 'PROBLEM CHILDREN'

If there is one exercise in our in-house seminars that can be somewhat problematical to run, it is the team task that goes as follows.

Decide what factors or combination of factors would cause a client to be classified as a 'problem child' account and would therefore be the subject of actions that could result in their returning to valued client status or alternatively the loss of their business.

So often when teams report back and we cut through the verbiage we are faced with the real answer that so long as the work is profitable then the firm will continue to work for any client. Anything for a quid! One client that we were recently working with clearly had a 'problem child' issue. A major client suddenly going bust had sounded alarm bells. In hindsight there had been warning signals but no one had wanted to take notice whilst the billing kept rolling in. They were ripe for this exercise.

When one (largely partner orientated) team came back with the answer that amounted to, "We'll do anything if it's profitable", a number of other people who were carrying out the work then challenged the real profitability of much of this work in which the firm was engaged. They countered that if all of the costs of dealing with some of their large 'problem child' clients were actually allocated to the clients concerned then the business would not only be high hassle, low level and unpleasant. It would also be totally unprofitable. The partner group heard the other point of view but clearly dismissed it.

As an observer it was apparent that the loss of this business to the firm would place too many partners in a dilemma. They and their practice areas had lots of work on their desks. The thought of bare desks and a feeling of little confidence in how to replace this work were issues that some clearly did not want to even consider, let alone confront. It was a missed opportunity to tackle an issue critical to the business and unfortunately sent out the message to the junior professionals that they had better be prepared to put up with anything that made even marginal profit for the firm.

Before looking at the different ways that a firm can choose to deal with 'problem children' clients it is worth pausing for a moment to take on board a cautionary note from Reichheld, again from his book *The Loyalty Effect*. He says, "Every company has some customers it is better off without. They're unprofitable, they no longer fit the company's offerings (or never did), and managing their farewells – especially if they *want* to leave – is no loss to anyone. The danger, of course, is that on the basis of inadequate information, the company will mistakenly identify potentially valuable customers as marginal or dispensible."

Whilst not suggesting a licence to make excuses for the retention of every unsuitable client, equally we should be careful not to throw the baby out with the bathwater. Using low fee income (for instance) as a metric does not provide us with any insight into a suspected 'problem child' client's potential fee income possibilities.

DEALING WITH 'PROBLEM CHILDREN' CLIENTS

We have to start off with an assumption. The assumption is that a firm has grasped the nettle and has concluded that it does have some clients that are, overall, problems to the business.

A 'problem child' relationship can, theoretically, go two ways. Looking at The PACE Pipeline model in Chapter 1 there are two arrows associated with the P5 Pruning segment. One arrow leads out of the segment and back into the market. This means that any action we take may result in the loss of the client for all time. The other arrow which lies between P4 and P5 has two heads.

In other words not only can a 'problem child' client emerge from what was once considered a valued client, but our actions can lead to a 'problem child' potentially being converted back into a valued client.

In dealing with 'problem children' clients our advice would be to adopt the same philosophy and position as the Managing Director of the consulting engineering practice that we referred to earlier in this chapter. In other words, do whatever is necessary to try to bring the relationship back into kilter but be prepared to accept that the actions may not succeed and that the relationship may terminate.

There are a number of alternatives that a firm can adopt in order to try to remedy a 'problem child' situation. The options are not interchangeable or equally applicable to every situation. Which ever way forward is chosen the firm must act with utter integrity and honesty.

Let the relationship wither

With this option the firm does the minimum to execute the work professionally but puts no effort into client management. The firm accepts that this 'planned neglect' will probably see the client won away by a competitor at some point. However, at no point should the firm behave in any way that would potentially damage the firm's reputation.

Have a 'be honest' meeting

This was the option chosen by the Managing Director of the engineering consultancy business. We confront the client in the most positive and professional way with the problems that the firm has in dealing with them and / or their work. Diplomacy backed by a firm resolve to see the situation improved to our satisfaction may see movement from the client – if they value our services. We have to be prepared, however, to agree not to agree and to a mutually accepted termination of the business relationship. We should always remain cordial.

Set minimum acceptable fees

If the problem is low volume / low revenue / low profitability per instruction, then we should consider setting a minimum fee level per instruction.

Delegate the client

To increase the profitability of work from a client, delegate the work – and the management of the relationship – to capable but more junior (and less expensive) people within the firm. If the client simply won't accept the new relationship then we may have to accept that they will take their business elsewhere.

Service at a distance

'Problem children' clients can often consume disproportionate amounts of management time with our senior people having to be regularly involved in meetings with client personnel – often at their premises. We need to insist that, except in the direst emergencies, communication will be by electronic means and that there will be a pre-defined escalation process – meaning that most situations can be handled and resolved by reasonably junior people. Again, we should be prepared to lose the client if they cannot accept this erosion of the service standards they have come to expect.

Pass to a partner organisation

The work that may be unprofitable to us or may not fit with our strategic direction, may be meat and drink to other firms that we know and trust. Be prepared to recommend that the client works in future with a trusted partner organisation. There may (or may not) be a financial consideration attached to this arrangement.

Sorry, no silver bullets.

At the end of the day all firms choose their own direction. If the decision is to do nothing about the issue of 'problem children' clients then that is the total prerogative of the management of the firm –with two caveats.

Firstly the people who make this decision should never be heard to refer to "bloody clients" – or any similar disparaging remark about the firm's client base.

Secondly they must be prepared to accept that the firm will probably never find enough time to pursue and win the prospective clients it dreams of.

WHERE TO GO FROM HERE

Where to go from here if you run a firm or have overall responsibility for marketing and business development

Insist that each part of your firm takes the time out to agree the parameters that define a 'problem child' client and, using these parameters, agree who their 'problem child' clients are.

Insist on seeing all of these outputs before any practice area takes action. A 'problem child' client of one part of the firm may be a valued client for another. You may have to intervene and adjudicate.

Where 'problem' children' clients are identified, insist that the practice area that maintains the main relationship with the client puts into place an action plan to resolve the situation.

Where to go from here if you run a business unit within a professional firm

Sit down with a group from your business unit and agree the parameters that define a 'problem child' client. By applying these parameters agree who your 'problem children' clients are.

Put in place an action plan with each of these 'problem children' clients that will see them either turned into valued clients once more or lead to them choosing to give their business – and problems – to other advisors.

Where to go from here if you are a marketing or business development professional working with fee-earners

Work with a part of your firm that has a real issue with the quality of its clients and the work that they provide. They will be more receptive to seeking solutions and to potentially grasping the tough nettles.

Talk with influential people within this part of the firm about the clients they would ideally like to work with and the work that they would ideally like to do. Discuss the barriers to achieving this, one of which will almost certainly be a lack of time for serious new business development activity.

Raise the subject of 'problem children' clients with these people and the conditions for 'lack of fit'. Encourage this part of the firm to truly identify its 'problem children' – clients that it is prepared to do something about.

Encourage the partners in this part of the firm to implement an action plan to begin to resolve their 'problem children' issue but in parallel support them in the construction and execution of a new business acquisition plan designed to bring in new, quality business.

Where to go from here if you are an individual practitioner within a professional firm

Look at the clients whose relationships you are responsible for. Do any of these deserve the label 'problem child'? If they do, then firstly work out a plan to generate new fee income that will replace that of your 'problem children'.

Begin implementing your plan and in parallel look at the options available and plan how to deal with your 'problem children'. Work could be a lot more pleasant and rewarding in future.

Chapter 7 **The Role of Marketing and Business Development Support**

THE TENSION BETWEEN MARKETING AND FEE-EARNERS

In the introduction to this book we made reference to marketing support people. Many marketers who have come from outside professional services have applied their expertise within this challenging environment. For some the chemistry has not been right and they have returned to the environment from which they came. However, many have stayed within the professions and as we commented in the introduction, there is a hard core of very seasoned marketers who are highly capable in the context of the professional services marketplace.

The main complaint that we hear from marketing support people is that they find it difficult to make their voices heard and that they feel that they are not always appreciated and valued by the fee-earners with whom they work.

When one speaks with fee-earners who appear to demonstrate this kind of behaviour toward marketers they talk about not being able to see exactly what value many of the marketing people bring to the firm. The cost line is clear to see but the contribution to fee income is indistinct.

In our experience most marketing support people within a firm get involved in two main aspects of work. One aspect is the construction and delivery of the firm's Corporate and Capability Marketing activities. They lead rebranding exercises, they are heavily involved in organising the firm's sponsorship and mass corporate entertainment events and they are responsible for brochure production. They are in charge of marketing communications and PR, they lead website development and they organise seminars. As we explained under the heading of Return on Investment in Chapter 3, because these activities are distant from clients and prospective clients it is difficult to measure their effectiveness in terms of their effect on client retention and acquisition and also fee income.

The second main aspect of work in which marketers become involved is proposal support. Too many marketers feel obliged to accept the flawed judgement of fee-earners that a particular piece of work should be pursued. As we examined in Chapter 4 they become part of the herd that is often blindly pursuing work that can never be won. Despite the most creative efforts of the marketing support people, particularly as they are often brought into the pitch process very late in the day and expected to perform miracles, the best the firm can achieve is a 'highly commended', as the odds-on favourite walks off with the trophy. So what value have they added?

Given the role that marketers have historically played within many firms it is not surprising that fee-earners see the marketing department as an overhead which adds nebulous value to the firm.

THE RISE OF THE BUSINESS DEVELOPMENT MANAGER

We believe that the role – and shape – of the marketing department is changing. We see one part of the department (let's call this Central Marketing) becoming responsible for all Corporate Marketing and most of the firm's Capability Marketing. A second part of the marketing department is then positioned within practice areas and market facing groups. This part of the marketing support team is responsible for the Capability Marketing activities that relate to the practice area in question plus the organisation and follow up of area-specific Contact Marketing and business development activities.

Over the past few years this second role has taken shape within a number of the more forward thinking and business development orientated firms. It is starting to show success both in terms of new business acquisition and also in respect of the stronger relationships that we see growing between the business development support people and the fee-earners within the firms that have adopted the practice. Most firms refer to this role as the Business Development Manager (BDM).

The BDM role, we believe, is a challenging and rewarding one. In it there is no place to hide. The relatively small group of fee-earners with whom the BDM is working closely on a day to day basis will be able to measure directly the contribution that that person is making. The role is not passive; it is active, with the BDM working in partnership with fee-earners. It represents an exciting development for marketers who can seize the opportunity to demonstrate a high return on the investment in their role.

The Role of the Business Development Manager

The accountabilities that we see for a Business Development Manager look something like the following.

•   Help fee-earners to clarify the selection criteria for prospective clients that the business unit is seeking to win in the future.

•   Manage the process of identifying the Defined Prospects that fit the profile.

- Construct (jointly with the fee-earners) the marketing and approach programme that will be used toward these prospects.

- Ensure that the programme is executed to plan.

- Be involved in (some of) these marketing and approach activities.

- Coach fee-earners in their roles in the marketing and approach activities.

- Prepare and coach fee-earners for their roles in early meetings with Defined Prospects.

- Participate in early meetings with Defined Prospects.

- De-brief and coach fee-earners in their execution of early meetings with Defined Prospects.

- Agree with fee-earners how they will continue their on-going approach to Qualified Prospects – with a view to winning an initial piece of work.

- Manage the process (with the aid of fee-earners) of constructing the business unit's Bluebird Checklist.

- Be the guardian of the Bluebird Checklist and act as devil's advocate for all proposal opportunities that are presented to the business unit.

- Act as coach to fee-earners when they propose and pitch for identified pieces of work from both prospective and current clients.

- Assist in the construction (and potentially the delivery) of the pitch and proposal – but not take responsibility for this.

- Take feedback from clients on reasons why proposals and pitches were won and lost and provide feedback to fee-earners.

- Assist fee-earners in the construction and execution of key client plans.

- Support fee-earners in their plans to market, sell and cross-sell their services to their clients.

- Assist fee-earners in the preparation for 'formal' client care meetings.

- Attend (and possibly contribute to) client care meetings.

- De-brief and coach fee-earners on their conduct of client care meetings.

Most of us know very quickly whether a coach has helped us or not. The Business Development Manager function (as we see the role) involves a high coaching element and therefore fee-earners will experience the added value that this person can bring in very short order. Equally if a person is not up to the job this will also be evident quickly.

Marketing supremos may worry that, with such a deep involvement in a particular practice area or market facing group, a BDM may go 'native'. Their concern is that the person may more quickly relate to the business unit with which they work rather than the marketing department.

This will almost certainly be the case. Where we have seen this type of BDM role evolving, the business unit heavily influences (for instance) the recruitment and selection process. The successful candidate is not allocated to their part of the firm. The business unit chooses whom they believe will fit and will contribute.

We do not believe that reorganising the marketing function is simply a case of taking the people who work in a firm's marketing function and splitting them into two groups – Central Marketing to the right, BDMs to the left! In many firms there are plenty of people who are well qualified to join the group on the right but we meet less people with the qualities to join the team on the left. Recruitment may well be necessary, which raises the question, what sort of person are we looking for?

Characteristics of a Business Development Manager

The individual who fills this role will need to have a reasonable understanding of marketing and business development – and ideally in the context of professional services. If we don't appear to be too hard and fast on this requirement, it is because we are not. These things are about knowledge and a bright person who is motivated to learn will acquire knowledge quickly enough.

What is much more important is that a person who is to fit the BDM role has the right motivations, attitudes, habits and aptitudes for the role. They come as part of the package once we employ someone. Taking our PACKASH (Personality and Motivation, Attitudes, Circumstances, Knowledge, Aptitudes, Skills, Habits) model, described in detail in our book *Managing Key Clients*, we would suggest that a firm should be looking for someone who would come close to the example below.

The 'built-in' motivational factors of achievement, responsibility, need for learning and goal orientation need to be high but these should ideally be accompanied by a low power motivation. This role is not about power – it is about influence. This is why the individual needs high levels of self esteem, verbal reasoning, persuasiveness and listening skills. Getting along with people is important therefore adaptability should be high and affiliation and sociability somewhat above average. Because the

Characteristics required to fulfil the role of Business Development Manager in a professional services firm

Need for challenge an achievement	1	2	3	4	5	6	●	8	9
Personal development – need for learning	1	2	3	4	5	6	●	8	9
Power need	1	●	3	4	5	6	7	8	9
Need for responsibility	1	2	3	4	5	6	●	8	9
Goal orientation	1	2	3	4	5	6	●	8	9
Dependence	1	2	3	4	●	6	7	8	9
Persistence and resilience	1	2	3	4	5	6	●	8	9
Self esteem	1	2	3	4	5	6	7	●	9
Mental energy	1	2	3	4	5	6	●	8	9
Work ethic	1	2	3	4	5	6	●	8	9
Personal organisation / orderliness	1	2	3	4	5	6	●	8	9
Technical bias	1	2	3	4	●	6	7	8	9
Long / short term orientation	1	2	3	4	●	6	7	8	9
Initiative and resourcefulnes	1	2	3	4	5	●	7	8	9
Affiliation and sociability	1	2	3	4	5	●	7	8	9
Adaptability	1	2	3	4	5	6	●	8	9
Analytical ability	1	2	3	4	5	6	●	8	9
Verbal reasoning	1	2	3	4	5	6	●	8	9
Persuasiveness	1	2	3	4	5	6	●	8	9
Listening skills	1	2	3	4	5	6	●	8	9

(1 – 9 scoring is based on the average distribution curve for the entire population)

individual will be working with many people whose discipline toward business development activities will not be high, the person should have strong personal organisation and high persistence and resilience.

At the same time we do not want this person to become bogged down in detail therefore we would look for only average technical bias and also a balance between long and short term thinking. Similarly we would suggest that the individual should be neither highly independent nor highly dependent on others and therefore someone who sits between these poles would be more suited to the role.

Does this ideal person exist? Almost certainly not – but it does at least provide a profile to work towards in order to find people to fill a key future role within the business development function of professional services firms.

PLANNING BDM ACTIVITY USING THE PACE PIPELINE MODEL

What should a BDM ultimately be seeking to achieve in his role? We would suggest that one aim would be to spend as much time as possible working alongside a group of professionals who really appreciate the BDM's knowledge and skills and who engage the BDM in helping them to retain and win business essential to the firm. The BDM should be trying to create his own highly satisfied client base of professionals in the same way that a professional is trying to create his own 'designer' client base. There are parallels in the two scenarios. For this reason we believe that BDMs should look to The PACE Pipeline model that we examined in Chapter 1, and reproduce below, and use this as a framework for structuring their activities.

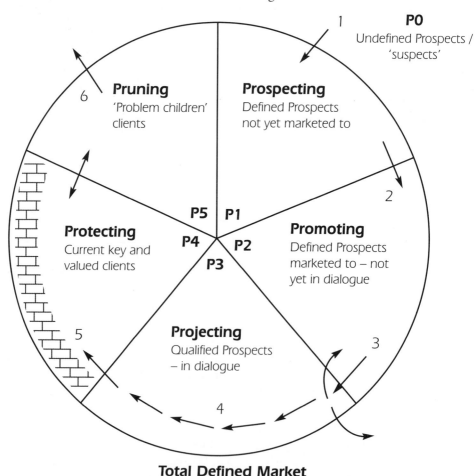

Total Defined Market

P5 – Pruning

The starting point for a BDM's thinking should probably begin in the P5 (Pruning) segment of the model where the activity is depicted by arrow(s) 6. Some BDMs spend too much of their time trying to support professionals who continually involve them in fruitless activity – particularly proposal support where it is clear from the outset that the percentages are stacked against the firm. Some can also be so extremely difficult to work with that they make the BDM's life a misery. The arrows related to activity 6 in The PACE Pipeline suggest two ways forward. We can return the 'problem child' client to become one of our valued clients or we can choose to lose the client altogether.

There is no point in the BDM complaining about the professionals with whom he works and then doing nothing about it. That is the equivalent to a fee-earner complaining about his clients yet continuing to tolerate their business and behaviour and doing nothing to change the shape of his client base. The BDM has to confront the situation. By the word 'confront' we do not suggest aggression. We are suggesting that the BDM needs to sit down, one on one, with the professional concerned and try to work through the issues, generated by the professional, that are causing the BDM to be less effective in his role.

Just as in the 'be honest' alternative which we examined in the previous chapter, the BDM should be seeking resolution and agreement to a way that the two parties can work together productively in the future. If this cannot be achieved then the BDM has to do whatever he can (within the rules of the firm in which he works) to ensure that when he is called upon by the 'problem child' professional in future, he is 'too busy' to support. 'Too busy' should mean that he is engaged in demonstrably more productive work elsewhere.

P1 – Prospecting

Rather than being reactive and 'on call', BDMs should be proactive. They should identify which professionals or which parts of the practice that they are not engaged with currently that they would like one day to have as their highly satisfied 'internal clients'. The selection criteria can be very simple. It may be that the 'Defined Prospect' fee-earner is very high profile and would be a terrific reference point for the BDM – a small 'win' for this person could help to build the BDM's reputation and credibility within the firm. It could be that the work that the professional is engaged in is highly profitable and the BDM believes that there is more of this type of work that the professional in question could win for others in the firm.

Whatever the selection criteria, the BDM should define a list of people with whom he is not working today, that he would wish to include as part of his 'designer internal client base' in the future.

P2 – Promoting

When it comes to the promoting segment and marketing activities, the BDM has the same task in relation to his professionals as those professionals have in relation to their prospective clients. The BDM has to make the professionals aware of his presence and he has to ensure that the fee-earners know exactly what he does (and doesn't) do.

Furthermore he has to try to convince the professionals with whom he has not worked previously, that he is exceptionally gifted in what he does.

We do not intend to do a re-run of Chapter 3 at this point. However, we find that most marketing departments in professional firms do next to nothing about promoting their services and capabilities.

Others do, however. Some marketing departments have created a section on the intranet and a 'mini brochure' to communicate 'exactly what we do'. Others have written up a few case studies of the successes that they have achieved with other fee-earners. Some offer lunchtime workshops on a particular business development issue of relevance and value to their internal clients and potential clients. This gives those potential clients some perspective on what it is like to work with the BDM concerned. It also helps to take potential 'internal clients' to the point where they 'believe that we can do it ...'

In short both BDMs and Central Marketing people should examine the list of marketing tools available and decide which ones have relevance and application in order to avoid the all too common shortcoming of failing to market marketing.

P3 – Projecting

This is where the BDM should be spending much of his time. There will always be an element of this time that is spent in being reactive to fee-earners' requests for 'immediate' support, but as we have pointed out earlier, this type of activity should not monopolise the BDMs time. Also, if the BDM is predominantly operating in reactive mode then he will nearly always be being drawn in to the 'back end' business development activities – typically the proposal. A good BDM can give most input and support at the early and mid stages of the selling process, helping the professionals to create a strong platform for a winning sales process and a winning proposal.

BDMs have to become proactive and seek to understand early the potential new business opportunities that their fee-earners see on the horizon. They then have to act as coaches to the professionals. They have to be able to analyse where the firm stands in the selling process and then advise as to what steps need to be taken and how they need to be taken in order to place the firm in a winning position.

The BDM should measure:
- How much of his time is spent working in the P3 segment?
- How much of this time is spent in reacting to fee-earners' requests and how much is dedicated to proactive efforts?
- How much of the total time in P3 activity is spent on 'back end' activities? (e.g. preparing and delivering proposals and pitch presentations.) How much is spent supporting in the early and mid stages of the business development process? (e.g. observing first meetings and coaching professionals in constructing their sales process.)

P4 – Protecting

Professionals rarely have a constant need for the support of BDMs. The requirement waxes and wanes in much the same way that a client does not constantly require a professional's services. In the case of the professional / client relationship a very fundamental piece of client care practice would be to keep in touch. This lets the client know that the professional is thinking about her and the proactive contact also gives the client the opportunity to flag up any impending issues where the professional's time and expertise may be required. This kind of early intelligence is far better than a last minute call from the client asking for an immediate response.

We would suggest that BDMs adopt this simple practice with the professionals with whom they work. A two minute telephone call is all that it takes. If the professional is tied up in work and hard to speak to, then a three line e-mail is a second best option.

Also BDMs could take a lesson from those fee-earners who use their best clients as reference points. Take the situation where a BDM has helped out a fee-earner and his intervention has been particularly useful and has helped the fee-earner to be more successful in his selling role. The professional is likely to thank him for the support given.

At this point it is an ideal time to say something along the following lines. "I'm glad that what I've been able to do has helped you so much. This is the kind of thing that I would like to do for more people in the practice area but some are more reluctant or sceptical. Could I ask you for something? Could I ask you to be a reference point for me? It would help me greatly if I meet a situation that is similar to the one we have been working on together recently and the professional is unsure of involving me. If I could ask the person to talk with you about your experience, would you be prepared to do that?"

How many highly satisfied professionals are likely to reply with a no? BDMs should be constantly developing their reference professionals and their advocates. This helps their credibility enormously and is a powerful marketing tool that helps them to create their 'designer internal client base'.

MANAGING THE CLIENT AND PROSPECT DATABASE

One of the tasks that Central Marketing should take overall responsibility for is managing the firm's database and contact management system. That is database – singular! Whilst BDMs may very quickly go native they should never be allowed to join forces with those fee-earners who believe that the firm's database doesn't do what they need it to do, and therefore conclude that they need to create one of their own.

If there is one area where many professional firms continue to look amateurish to their clients and prospective clients it is in the construction and use of their database. We have heard scores of damning anecdotes that could have been avoided if the firm in question had a single central database that people believed in, used and consulted. Probably the worst story we have been told was the situation where two offices of a consulting engineering business were bidding against each other – neither realising who they were in competition with. Worse was to come as their bids were the two that reached the shortlist. Needless to say they were very similar so the client played one off against the other in a Dutch auction in order to reduce the price. It was only after one office won the business, at a ridiculous price, that it came to light what had happened.

Lots of firms struggle to get fee-earners to submit billing information so it is unrealistic to expect that these same fee-earners are going to spend hours of their time making database entries. However, there is an education process required here in order that fee-earners realise the importance and value of an accurate database to their business unit and to the firm as a whole.

What is needed is a joint effort in order that the necessary, updated information reaches the central database. Secretaries have a vital role in this. They have the IT and keyboard skills to do most of this work swiftly. After any significant contact that a fee-earner has with a client, a secretary – who is signed on to the importance of the database – could simply ask, "Anything for the database?" This would be a prompt for the fee-earner to quickly verbally download any changes that he has been made aware of within the client's organisation or to post a one line file note on his latest exchange with the client.

Within a practice area that has adopted a BDM, then this person should be the custodian of the database, encouraging and cajoling both fee-earners and support staff to continually keep it alive and up to date.

Keeping the database alive is so important in order that the firm does not look stupid to its clients. On telephoning a client or prospective client about an impending issue the last thing that a professional wants to hear is, "We are dealing with this internally. I told the chap from your firm who rang me last week that this is what we planned. I also told your Client Partner when we had lunch together last month. Don't you people ever talk to each other?"

How much damage can these incidents do? And, particularly in large firms with multiple practice areas and office locations and a discredited and worthless database, they happen all of the time.

We do have some sympathy with practice area or office heads who, in frustration at the quality of the overall firm's database decide to create their own. However local and partial databases are a temporary fix and always create longer term problems for the firm as a whole.

The only long term solution is for the firm to invest in the best database or CRM system that it possibly can. Time should be spent at the outset to ensure that this system meets as closely as possible, the needs of the various constituents who will use, and contribute to the upkeep of, the information it contains. Central Marketing should coordinate this activity and be a thorn in the side of the firm's management team if the business's client and prospect database is not capable of servicing the organisation's needs.

WHERE TO GO FROM HERE

Where to go from here if you run a firm or have overall responsibility for marketing and business development

Look at the people employed in your marketing support team. How many are engaged principally in a Central Marketing role and how many are in a Business Development Manager type of role? Are you satisfied that this current mix serves your business well? If not then ensure that the mix of resources is rebalanced.

Ensure the role of your BDMs is clear and make sure your BDMs have the capabilities and confidence to carry out their roles effectively. Check that each BDM's Pipeline plans are in place and working and review their effects regularly. Support the BDMs in their planned interactions with fee-earners.

Ask a cross section of people in your firm if your current database and CRM system satisfies their needs in respect of being an aid to marketing and business development. If the shortcomings seem mainly minor then live with this or make changes if they don't cost too much. No database is perfect for everyone. If, on the other hand, your client and prospective client database is badly flawed or limited then begin the process of planning for the construction and introduction of a new one.

Where to go from here if you run a business unit within a professional firm

Try to ensure that you employ a really good Business Development Manager in your business unit. He or she will be worth their weight in gold. Understand the BDM's Pipeline plans and provide visible support to his efforts.

Before you complain that your firm's current database is useless, have a word with someone in marketing or IT who fully understands its functionality. Sometimes discredited databases can provide more functionality than people believe. Many problems can lie principally with uneducated users.

Don't be tempted to start your own database. You will simply become part of the problem.

If your firm's database really does have shortcomings then join the lobby group seeking an upgrade. You will probably be in good company. Sometimes a firm's most senior people do not realise the day to day problems that a poor database causes the average professional within the firm so sometimes it takes many voices acting in concert to make them hear.

Where to go from here if you are a marketing or business development professional working with fee-earners

Look at what type of role you are best suited for today. Is it a Central Marketing type of role with a focus on firm wide Corporate and Capability Marketing activities or are you better cut out for a Business Development Manager type of role?

If you have a yearning to change or develop your role (perhaps more toward the Business Development Manager role) then seek out training and development programmes that will give you the kinds of knowledge and skills that you will need in the future. Consider raising the subject of the shape of your future role with those who run the firm or those who have overall responsibility for marketing.

If you are employed in a BDM role then look at using The PACE Pipeline model as a basis for structuring your activity. Re-examine the ideas contained under the heading *Planning BDM activity using The PACE Pipeline model.*

If the firm's database does not provide what management, fee-earners, marketers and support people require, begin to create a list of the functionalities that all these four constituent groups are looking for. At some point the firm will need to invest in a new database and a considered list of requirements, compiled over a period of time will be an invaluable asset in beginning the search for a new system.

Where to go from here if you are an individual practitioner within a professional firm

Look at the activities that you will need to get involved in over the next year in order to maintain and build your Pipeline. Then look at the marketing and business development support people employed by the firm. Try to draw your support from the right type of person. Central Marketing types won't be of much use in a business development scenario and business development types won't be much interested in Central Marketing sorts of activities.

If you feel that your firm's database hinders your marketing and business development efforts then add your voice to that of those seeking change. As suggested earlier however, before you complain, have a word with someone in marketing or IT who understands fully its functionality.

BRITAIN'S RAILWAYS AT WAR
1939 to 1945
by Alan Earnshaw

DESIGNED BY BARNABUS
From an original idea by Derek Huntriss

Printed by Century Litho, Penryn, Cornwall
Bound by Booth Bookbinders, Penryn, Cornwall

ISBN 0–906899–33–8
First published 1989

Published by:

ATLANTIC TRANSPORT PUBLISHERS

**Waterside House, Falmouth Road,
Penryn, Cornwall TR10 8BE, England.**

Atlantic

Front Cover: *The face of railways at war, Liverpool Street Station in September 1939, with the first of the evacuees. LNER class B12, No 8556 simmers in the late-summer sun, as the driver spends a few moments with the children 'to take their mind off things'.*

Rear Cover, Bottom Right: *During the six years of war a large proportion of military supplies were conveyed by rail from small parcels to very large objects like guns and tanks (armoured fighting vehicles or AFVs). Here a train of Cromwell tanks is being unloaded from specially constructed flat wagons, telegraphic code 'Warflat'. Larger tanks were conveyed on wagons with a dropped 'well' between the bogies to give additional height (code Warwell). These trains ran as 'out of gauge' loads under special signalling regulations. The location is Winchester City on 2nd September 1944 and this scene was a follow up to the D-Day invasion of France.* PHOTO: NATIONAL RAILWAY MUSEUM COLLECTION

Rear Cover, Top: *Some of the German air raids were during daylight hours especially on the East Coast. This scene at Middlesborough was one such raid when an empty train was damaged and the station roof partially destroyed. In spite of the apparent serious state of the locomotive Class VI 2-6-2T No 416, it was repaired and returned to traffic* PHOTO: NATIONAL RAILWAY MUSEUM COLLECTION

Rear Cover, Bottom Left: *Going home, amidst sunshine and shadows, at King's Cross.*

Title Page: *A military guard at Copenhagen Tunnel watches as LNER class V2, No 4826 heads north from London on December 1st 1939. Guarding the railways was an early priority for the Government, as stories abounded of fifth columnists, or enemy parachutists dressed as nuns riding bikes.*

Top Left: *Though horse power was generally outdated in WW2, it was still used in some theatres of war. Here mules for a mountain battery are loaded at the ex-LNWR station at Weedon on April 22nd 1942. The station saw a considerable amount of horse traffic, due to its proximity to the Army Equestrian Centre.*

Bottom Left: *A variety of equipment was supplied by railway works for use by the British Expeditionary Force. On May 23rd 1940 a train of gun-limbers are ready to leave the Birmingham Railway Carriage and Wagon Co works.*

Introduction

No conflict which involves the taking of human life should ever be glorified, but those periods of war which have affected our country have a fascinating history. This is particularly so in the field of transport, when vast armies, their machinery and equipment had to be moved suddenly and expeditiously from one part of the country to another. Perhaps one of the earliest visual records of such movement is recorded in the Bayeux Tapestry, which shows King Harold's march from Stamford Bridge to Hastings in the autumn of 1066.

Almost nine hundred years later the German armies were poised to invade Britain, the island fortress, which stood alone against the might of the Hitler war machine. Though isolated, and soaking up the punishment thrown against her, help came from the Empire, and the United States. Along her vital arteries, the roads and railways, this overseas aid flowed to a besieged nation. However, Britain's roads at the time were often poor, winding legacies of the days of horse and cart, a method of transport still to some extent employed in rural areas. So the only means of rapid transport that existed to move men, munitions and machinery were Britain's railways.

At the outbreak of war in September 1939, the railways were generally in excellent order. There were over 37,000 miles of running lines, which had seen the vast sum of £315,500,000 spent on their development in the preceding decade. The best train services were the most modern in the world, and only the year before *Mallard* had taken the world speed record for a steam powered locomotive. Not only the LNER, but on the Southern, Great Western and LMS too, many locomotives and much coaching stock had been built to the most modern designs. If Britain's politicians or army was not fully equipped for the outbreak of war, its railways were.

Beginning with the formation of a Railway Executive in September 1939, the traffic on each of the big four companies, London Passenger Transport, and several minor railways came under central control. Collectively the Executive and the railways took Britain through the war.

Above: *Just a few weeks before Dunkirk, troops leave for France. Chalked messages on the carriage sides being typical of the farewell scenes on stations around the country.*

It all began with the evacuation of children from major cities, followed by the mobilisation of the British Expeditionary Force, who were promptly embarked for France and the Low Countries. Their hasty retreat from Dunkirk the following year was the prelude for the start of the German offensive on Britain. It began with the Battle of Britain, and led into the blitz, through which time the railways moved men and supplies essential for the country's independence. As the tide of war changed, so did the role of the railways which saw the embarkation of the 1st Army for North Africa, and the movement of 'Operation Overlord' forces prior to D-Day. In the end the railways repatriated the fighting men, re-uniting them with their families; but sadly many thousands who had said goodbye to their loved ones on a crowded station platform, never did return.

This pictorial history is but a brief glimpse of those troubled times. In using high quality press photographs, we have been able to portray almost every aspect of life on the working railways of Britain during the war years, providing a unique glimpse at the other side of railways. The build up to the war, evacuation of children from cities, anti-gas and air raid precautions are all covered, whilst bomb damage, underground tube shelters and late running show the effects on civilian railways in war. How the railways were kept running, particularly with women employees, is shown in context with the exceptional increase in freight and armament traffic. A unique view is also afforded of the lesser known side of railway operations in the war, including catering, luggage, and hospital trains.

Finally, the story is concluded with sections on railway workshops, locomotives for abroad, and main-line accidents. However, it should be said that this is not a picture book about trains, but rather a look at how railways played a vital role in the social history of the period 1939 to 1945.

All photographs courtesy of Keystone Library unless otherwise credited.

Air raid precautions

The vast railway marshalling yards, key junctions and major stations became places of strategic importance and thus susceptible to enemy attack. During World War I, a number of raids were made on Britain's railway installations by the German Zeppelin airships. With more modern aircraft at its disposal, the Luftwaffe had ample capacity to inflict severe damage upon the railways, as had been evidenced in Poland, France and the Low Countries at the start of the war.

Air raid precautions were at first quite simple, involving a general blackout and the provision of fire buckets. The real threat was considered to be gas, and all railway crews were issued with gas masks. They were also amongst the first civilians provided with steel helmets, to offer protection from flying shrapnel.

Signalmen were given small steel cabinets in which they could enclose

Above: *To combat fire at railway installations, the GWR formed three mobile fire-fighting trains. Crewed by eight men, they were manned 24 hours a day, sleeping and eating accommodation being provided on the train.*

Left: *By February 28th 1941 the railway 'fire-men' had become totally proficient, but still continued to practise; as is shown in this view with crews unloading trailer-pumps from a Covered Carriage Truck (CCT) using block and tackle.*

Opposite: *To offer protection to its footplate crews, the Southern Railway had issued them all with steel helmets by September 18th 1939.*

themselves during an air raid. These were found to be necessary after a signalman was killed by flying glass in his box in the Midlands. Being behind a large body of glass, he had been killed by the blast of a bomb a quarter of a mile away; but more seriously his death resulted in an accident to a train under his control. Although only two passengers were actually hurt in the derailment, it resulted in a blockage of a major junction which took two days to clear with all the attendant delays to traffic. Generally the shelters were not liked, and most signalmen resorted to them only when bombs were falling in the immediate vicinity.

Fire alarms and air-raid warning gongs were established in railway yards, where the civilian sirens were not easily heard due to the background noise. These alarms were usually under the care of the yard foreman or the station master, and only on his instructions could they be sounded. At some establishments it was common to sound the alarm much later than the civilian siren, in order to keep the men working right up to the last possible moment before an attack. During the hours of darkness, look-outs were stationed in the railway yards, often on signal gantries or up yard lamps, from where they could have a commanding view of the establishment they were pro-tecting – watching out for attacking aircraft or fires which might be started. In all, 170,000 railwaymen and women received ARP training in the first four years of war.

Fire-fighting was yet another specialised task that was also taught to railwaymen; in all, 73 special fire-fighting trains were constructed and stationed at key points outside major towns and cities, to be brought into use in any case of emergency. On the Southern Railway, orders were given for several of these trains to be made up; these were to comprise six old locomotive tenders specially converted as water carriers, a coach providing sleeping and living accommodation for eight men, a covered carriage truck (CCT) holding the pumps, and a stores van carrying auxiliary fire-fighting equipment. Similarly the GWR developed its own fire-fighting trains, but preferred to concentrate on road trailer pumps, capable of delivering 150 gallons

On no account
must this gong be
sounded other than
for air raid warning

of water per minute. However the off-loading of these vehicles away from stations proved to be both difficult and time consuming, until block and tackle equipment was fitted to the vans for use where no platform existed.

In many goods yards, and alongside other major railway centres, emergency dams were constructed as static water points, most with a capacity of around 100,000 gallons. Special hydrants were constructed to take supplies from locomotive watering facilities such as water cranes, parachute tanks and tank houses. Everywhere, it became common practice to distribute large numbers of sand-buckets, whilst shunting engines and guards vans were equipped with hose-pipes and stirrup pumps to enable crews to deal with fires where the brigade engines couldn't reach.

Left: *King's Cross shed on the LNER was one of the company's most important depots. Consequently very serious measures were taken to protect both it and its staff from air attack. High-pitched metallic gongs are seen being erected on November 26th 1939, after it was found that ordinary alarms could not be heard over the noise of locomotives. Also of interest are the hand-bell and rattle contained in the cabinet below. The practice of painting white lines on the corners of buildings became common after the introduction of the black-out.*

Top Right: *Following the signal box tragedy in the Midlands, the LMS issued a tall steel cabinet to many of their boxes. This Air Raid Precaution (ARP) cabinet was designed to offer protection from flying shards of glass during bombing raids; however they became irreverently known as 'tin coffins' and many were used for little more than storage lockers.*

Bottom Right: *In 1937 the LMS combined secretly with the Home Office to build a special ARP train at the Wolverton Works. It first appeared in the autumn containing two coaches equipped with de-contaminating equipment, and coaches fitted out as ARP training centres. It became known as the 'yellow train' and is seen here at Euston with the guard wearing a gas mask and special gloves.*

The major precaution was of course the blackout, and some extraordinary lengths were taken to ensure the blackout was maintained. In some cases coach windows were completely painted out, whilst in others a narrow strip was painted down the sides covering the gap on either side of the blind. Low watt or blue bulbs were placed in coach compartment lights, and lineside braziers and fog 'devils' were encapsulated in metal containers; but despite all precautions, some trains were still easily spotted at night. My grandparents' house was almost a mile away from the ex-LNWR Standedge line, yet I am told that the glow from the chimneys could quite easily be identified as locomotives laboured toward the summit. It was perhaps inevitable that no blackout could be totally enforced where live steam was concerned, but all in all

Left: *Roof spotting and fire watching became an important part of home defence, and despite the fact that it involved sitting in a lonely exposed position in all weathers, hundreds of men did their bit every night of the year. As he climbs to his 'Jim Crow' nest at Camden Shed on November 29th 1940, this LMS spotter has a commanding view of Royal Scot 4-6-0 No 6119* Lancashire Fusilier, *with Chalk Farm Station to the rear.*

Opposite Top: *The all important black-out was rigorously enforced, particularly on the railways. Low watt bulbs were placed in carriage lights, and shades then placed around them. On top of this, the windows were often painted black, as is shown in this view taken at Ashford in September 1939.*

Opposite Bottom: *Where entire carriage windows were to be blacked-out it wasn't sufficient to paint just a single side, as this could become abraded in the course of normal daily use – letting light through as a result. Accordingly, both inside and outside were painted, as is evidenced at the Derby carriage works, where these withdrawn dining cars are receiving attention. This black-out was applied a month after the outbreak of war, when the dining cars had been withdrawn. However, they were re-introduced on October 12th 1939, and this work shows the preparation for that return to service.*

the railways made a determined effort to conceal themselves.

Unfortunately a number of lives were lost in Britain's railway yards and engine sheds during the war, not by enemy attack, but by the measures taken to prevent them. Railway installations are notoriously dangerous places even in daylight, becoming even worse in the hours of darkness with just dim lighting being provided for safety reasons. However all such lighting was extinguished during the war, and consequently hazards abounded to trap the unfamiliar or the unwary. A number of deaths are recorded where railwaymen (and women) fell into obstacles like ash pits, turntable wells, and inspection pits. Other instances relate of workers being run over or crushed during shunting operations in the goods yards. To help prevent such accidents corners of buildings and the edge of pits were painted white which aided visibility. In one region there was an experiment with painting wagon buffers white, though due to the nature of their use were found to be in constant need of re-painting and the idea was abandoned.

Allied to air raid precautions were the efforts made to guard key railway centres,

Below: *A copy of the Air Raid Precaution notices which were pasted in the carriages, as seen on the coach window pictured above.*

ARP(R)

AIR RAID PRECAUTIONS
INSTRUCTIONS TO PASSENGERS

If an air raid occurs while you are in the train:

1. Do NOT attempt to leave the train if it stops AWAY FROM A STATION unless requested by the guard to do so. You are safer where you are.

2. Pull the blinds down both by day and night, as a protection against flying glass.

3. If room is available lie down on the floor.

Left: *Black-out rules were also enforced in railway installations like stations, goods depots and signal-boxes. These were perhaps the most awkward to control, as signalmen needed an unobstructed view of the lines under their control, however black-out curtains were still provided, as is shown in the all-electric box at Waterloo.*

Below: *Much more difficult to 'black-out' were the braziers, and 'fog-devils' used on the lineside. Attempts were made to disguise the light emission from these types of apparatus by encapsulating them in metal containers. With the increasing problems caused by fog and the black-out, these items were much in demand in the winter of 1939-40; as a result about 250 were converted on the LMS alone in December 1939.*

junctions and tunnels where, at the outbreak of the war, regular soldiers or reservists appeared on sentry duty. In due course these men were moved elsewhere, as more detachments of local defence volunteers were established. These units eventually became known as the Home Guard and railway employees played an important role in the movement, with around 90,000 workers becoming part-time soldiers. If this number is added to the 170,000 employed in ARP duties, it comes to a staggering total of 260,000 or about half the total workforce. During the course of their daily work, railwaymen were often called upon to face additional perils, particularly while handling live ammunition. In all these activities the railwaymen exhibited acts of devotion, and in a number of cases went much further and showed courage above and beyond the call of duty. Not only were these acts of courage recognised by the railway companies, but in many instances medals were awarded including the George Cross, the George Medal, and the British Empire Medal.

Bomb damage

Despite all the precautions, the inevitable still happened, and the railway network suffered some quite major damage. All over the British Isles, railway installations were affected. The later tactics of 'train-busting' employed by RAF and USAF fighter pilots using Hurricane, Mustang and Kittihawk aircraft was not successfully copied by the Luftwaffe except for occasional and seemingly haphazard attacks in the southern counties. Therefore the opportunity of semi-paralysing the nation through systematic concentration on its railways, was one which the German High Command apparently overlooked. Yet Britain, stretched as it was in the early years of the war, had become highly dependent on its railway network; had the latter been systematically attacked, then conceivably a German invasion might have succeeded.

In fact Britain had one major asset; a multitude of routes, its legacy from the pre-grouping days. This plethora of alternatives gave the Railway Executive a variety of options for re-routing trains away from damage affected areas. Therefore, lines which had almost been a virtual liability in the pre-war years were now proving to be of vital strategic

Top: *In the course of World War II, over 12,000 tons of high explosive was dropped on London, six times more than any other provincial city. Almost half the country's 60,595 civilian dead were killed in the London region, with many more injured. Damage to railway installations was therefore inevitable, as exemplified by this view of the damage caused at Liverpool Street on the night of September 8th 1940.*

Bottom: *It was not only static targets that were at danger, as is portrayed by this view near Ingatestone. The train was travelling between Shenfield and Ingatestone when the track in front of it received a direct hit. As the train was travelling at the compulsory 20mph speed limit during air raids, there were no fatalities or serious injury. Considerable damage was caused to both locomotive and stock when it fell into the resulting bomb crater.*

importance. When aerial attack occurred, whether by incendiary devices, land mines or bombs, the various regional committees of the Executive usually had a variety of choices at their disposal, and could often re-route trains without causing major delays.

Even so, damage frequently occurred where no alternative routes were possible, particularly in large city terminal stations, where the Executive had to effect speedy repairs. A rapid repair

organisation was established in the early months of the war and within a short period had become so efficient that it could achieve amazing results. Main line tracks were repaired and restored to full running in a few hours, whilst bridges could be replaced within a day. To achieve this, permanent breakdown crews were put on stand-by at key centres, whilst prefabricated bridge spans, signal-box kits, and other repair materials were located at important junctions on the

Above: *In a daylight raid on 10th May 1941, the damage to St Pancras Station looks pretty serious. Despite the apparent devastation, trains were running again inside 9 hours.*

outskirts of towns and cities. When an attack resulted in damage, the repair teams swung into action, the work often commencing before the 'all-clear' was sounded. Even so, some major tasks had to be left as they were, or in a patched up condition until well after the war.

In a daylight raid on a London station, the surface platforms, and the connecting underground station were badly damaged; despite the apparent devastation, trains were again running through inside nine hours. The following day, a repaired station, complete with a new booking office was re-opened. Elsewhere in the city a vitally important station was so badly damaged, that an electric train had been blown off its track onto the platforms. All the running lines in and out of the station were either destroyed or blocked, but within 24 hours normal service had been resumed.

Damage was not limited to the major cities like London, Birmingham and Glasgow; small towns like Whitby also suffered, as did village stations and isolated sections of railway, hit by sneak German 'tip and run' raids. However, whether it was in a large city or in a rural location, the railways were quickly repaired – all part of the great effort to keep the nation's vital communications open.

Below: *One week later, the scene has been transformed. LMS railway engineers have repaired the damaged platforms, the famous single span roof remains almost undamaged. For security reasons, neither of these pictures were released to the press until 26th August 1942.*

Evacuees

The most moving sights on railway stations during World War II were the pitiful groups of children, lonely and bemused, walking around with little cardboard labels identifying both them and their luggage as evacuees. The consequences of a mass evacuation with heart-rending scenes of parting and fretful children in railway stations, may well be looked on as just one of the sad faces of a country at war. However, in social terms it could be said that the whole evacuation programme was an unmitigated disaster.

The Government had anticipated that bombs would begin falling as soon as war was declared, and consequently began the evacuation of children, pregnant women and the elderly on Friday September 1st 1939. All the stations of the great cities were swamped with thousands of people, who had been advised to seek refuge in the countryside or smaller towns. The fact that bombs did not fall was no fault of the Government, but the problems caused by the extreme measures it had taken fell upon the railways to sort out.

An estimated 3,500,000 evacuees were expected, but barely a third of that number arrived at the stations. Those that did arrive came in vast surges, usually early in the day congesting the platforms and waiting rooms. This threw the railway organisation into disarray, with all the carefully co-ordinated plans going out of the window. As there was no Government organisation to clear up the mess, it was left to station officials to clear the crowds the best way they could. In a large number of cases this was accomplished by loading people on to the first train to come into the station, regardless of either it or its passengers' actual destination.

In terms of a railway operation it worked well, with over 800,000 children alone being moved in three days, without anyone getting killed, injured or even lost. In social terms it was a disaster, with bewildered station-masters and billeting officers sorting out the chaos at the other end. Stations where 300 children were expected would receive but a few dozen, whilst those with no plans for evacuees could receive up to 500, who in turn became dependent on the good will of local people for a bed for the night.

Another problem was experienced in the type of some of the stock employed, with children (who frequently need the toilet) often being packed into non-corridor trains. This was exacerbated by the fact that journeys which usually took an hour could take anything up to five times longer. For example one train from London to Somerset was forced to terminate in Berkshire when the plaintive cries of the young passengers could be ignored no longer.

Evacuee traffic continued through the war, with many unable to settle away

from the big cities returning home after a few days, then fleeing again when prolonged periods of enemy attack began. Added to this, there were the occasional return trips home for holidays, funerals, and family gatherings; in short, a tide of human flotsam ebbing and flowing between city life and safety throughout the dark days of war.

Opposite: *If every boy's dream was to become an engine driver, then those pictured on this unidentified LNER class A4 Pacific in 1939 must have had the thrill of a lifetime. The compassion of railway employees for the evacuees was frequently in evidence as railwaymen showed their precious charges to children facing an uncertain future.*

Below: *Children evacuated from the big cities were not away from home all the time and at certain times of the year were re-united with their families. This Christmas scene at Waterloo Station in 1944 was therefore a familiar one to travellers of the day.*

Right: *With the collapse of France in 1940, the coastal areas of South-East England were no longer considered to be safe for the refugees from London. Some 48,000 children had to be uprooted once more, and were transported away by 70 trains which headed for destinations on the GWR and LMS. Once more this traumatic upheaval was eased by railway staff, as is shown in this view at an unidentified Southern Railway station.*

The threat of gas

It may seem strange to relate that the all consuming fear in the early days of the war was the threat of gas attack. This pathological fear stemmed, not from some alarmist official, but from evidence existing in every town, city and village. Almost everyone knew about someone who had been killed, or disabled by the gas attacks employed by the Germans in World War I. Mustard gas was one of the most terrible, which left survivors blind or with damaged lungs; so twenty years on from the armistice, horrible reminders of this abhorent form of warfare abounded.

The first anti-gas tactics were formulated long before the start of the war, a result of the Air Raid Precautions Department training programme which commenced in 1935. By January 1937, the first civilian gas masks became available, though these offered little comfort to women with elaborate hair-styles and make up, nor to men with beards. On the

Above: *The anti-gas and decontamination trains introduced by the GWR, were kept at constant readiness throughout the war with crews adhering to fixed training schedules. The mustard coloured coaches are shown here with crews practising connecting hoses to fill water tanks, essential for the operation of the hot and cold showers in the decontamination coach.*

Right: *Meanwhile on the LNER, ARP and anti-gas training was given to employees in all avenues of the railway service. This particular instruction is provided in a converted first class Gresley LNER dining car. The coach entered service on August 17th 1938, and is seen at King's Cross station during the first lecture.*

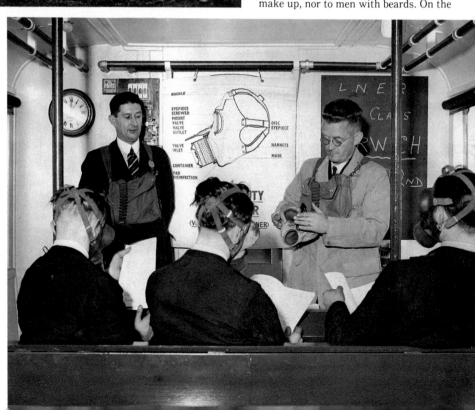

other hand, many children relished wearing them, thanks to being told that it made them look like 'Mickey Mouse'.

The grim necessity of anti-gas measures was impressed on all railway employees, and a fine was imposed by one division on the LMS from November 1937 for men failing to carry a gas mask when they signed on for duty. Whether or not this practice became universal, is not known, but by 1938 training began in earnest. At first railwaymen training in ARP duties were exposed to the smell of mustard, musty hay, pear-drops and geraniums. This was followed by exposure to tear-gas in a sealed room, and finally by giving them small whiffs of the actual gasses.

To further combat the danger, the railways formulated a much stronger strategy for dealing with gas attack by introducing special decontamination and de-gassing trains. Some 47 special cleansing vans were converted to provide facilities for areas where no decontamination equipment existed, or where existing arrangements were inadequate. Each van was provided with an air-lock, leading to a zinc lined shower-room, a third section was provided as a dressing room with fresh clothing. In addition to normal blackout, the vans were also provided with blast-proof windows.

It was considered that even though the Germans had not used gas in their earlier attacks, it was extremely likely that it would be employed at some later stage. Indeed, in several attacks in 1944 some of the V bomb warheads contained gas as opposed to high-explosives. Though this was purely a means to demoralise the civilian population, and the gas was quite ineffective and dissipated quite quickly, the threat was taken seriously and anti-gas measures were retained until the final days of the war. Even as late as January 1945 details of training in such precautions continued to be recorded by the railway companies.

Right: *Even at a late stage in the war, the threat of gas was still paramount and railway employees were impressed into the reality of working under gas-attack situations. In September 1943 a Southern Railway breakdown gang, looking more like deep sea divers, exercise somewhere in Kent.*

In the tube

The most vivid pictures of the London blitz are those of the deep underground shelters afforded by the railway system of the London Passenger Transport Board – the tube. At this point of time it might seem incredible to relate that at first the government tried to discourage their use, fearing the development of a 'shelter mind', with a population burrowing ever deeper to escape the rain of bombs. This attitude was overcome by people buying the cheapest possible ticket, officially entering as passengers, but in reality becoming shelterers. Eventually the Government was forced to succumb to popular pressure, and in all seventy-nine tube stations were provided as shelter for between 75,000 and 100,000 Londoners.

In fact several tube stations (particularly the older ones) were not very safe as they were located just below street level. At Balham one bomb actually penetrated the station where around 600 had sought refuge. Many were killed outright, with even more being drowned when a water main shattered. Water was in fact a major concern for LPTB engineers, who feared flooding of the system, by the Thames. To overcome this problem a series of floodgates were constructed at strategic points around the system, allowing the facility to seal off sections of the system in case the river broke through.

At certain stations bunks were available by reservation, as were floor spaces, but generally it was on a first come – first served basis. As a consequence, a pattern soon emerged which lasted until the last V2 'Flying Bomb' landed on London in 1945. Usually an older child would arrive first, around

school closing time, and armed with bedding and the like would proceed to stake out their family's space. The first choice were the platforms at the deeper levels, and inevitably this created congestion in the latter part of the day. To ensure free running of trains, and access for the true passengers, LPTB insisted in painting a white line 8ft from the platform edge. In this space, no bedding or baggage could be put down until after 7.30pm, after this the distance between sleeping area and platform edge was reduced to 4ft.

Despite all the camaraderie, the sing-songs, and the community spirit, the tube shelters were not the most glamorous of places. Once the 'all-clear' was sounded people left as quickly as they could,

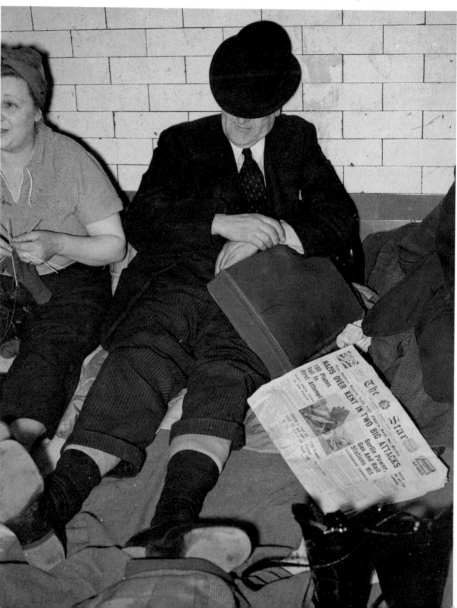

leaving behind huge piles of rubbish, including human and animal excretia. A few bombed-out families made semi-permanent homes in the 'dead-end' stations on the Liverpool St extension, however, the vast majority were glad to quickly escape from the dirty, draughty, lice-infested shelters.

Opposite Right: *Life in the tube was one of the great social levellers of all time, with the middle and working classes coming into intimate contact. They were not the cleanest of places, but the squalor and dirt below ground was much to be preferred to Herr Hitler's bombs above. This view in Aldwych Station with the bowler hat, the head scarf, and paper headlines says it all.*

Opposite Left: *Aldwych was a shelter where concerts were provided to while away the long evenings. It was rather untypical in that during the war, services to the station had been withdrawn, so the track area could also be used for a variety of activities like concerts and shows which were provided by theatre companies, and organisations like ENSA. To provide a stage, the platform was used, and the audience sat on the trackbed – naturally the current had been disconnected!*

Top Right: *Each afternoon six 'Tube Refreshment Specials' left individual depots, like this 4-car pre-1938 set at Cockfosters Depot on December 12th 1940. They carried around seven tons of food and refreshments, and it is significant that the train pictured here is on the line adjacent to the doorway leading to the depot canteen. The specials ran on the Bakerloo, Central, Northern and Piccadilly lines and supplied 134 canteens which served the 79 tube (and one Southern Railway) underground shelters. Every night 1,000 women worked on the service which was run on a non-profitmaking basis. Services began in 1940 and ran until 1942, but were resumed in 1943 after the commencement of the flying bomb attacks.*

Right: *On September 11th 1939, the LPTB announced the immediate closure of the Northern line between Kennington and Strand, and between Moorgate and London Bridge. This involved closing 19 stations, whilst engineers installed a series of floodgates to protect the system in case the bed of the River Thames was damaged by bomb attack.*

Running late

At every station posters on hoardings cried down 'IS YOUR JOURNEY REALLY NECESSARY', to which most travellers must have answered 'yes', for never were the passenger services so well patronised. People were packed in, completely beyond the capacity of the trains arriving to transport them: soldiers, sailors, airmen, and merchant navy crews, going home on leave or setting off for new postings, workers travelling hundreds of miles to new factories where they had been directed by the Ministry of Labour, normal commuters, and even car-owners forced on to the trains by petrol shortages.

So great was the strain, that trains could not hope to keep to time schedules. More time was added to journeys when threatened air-raids forced trains to pull into stations, for passengers to seek shelter if necessary. On top of this the actual bomb damage which did occur resulted in monumental delays. Commuters travelling into London from the suburbs, could find themselves spending as long in the train as they did at work, whilst cross-country journeys

Above: *Even in the darkest days of war, some people managed to escape from the cities to take a few days holiday, either in the country or by the sea. This traffic added even more pressure to a railway system bursting at the seams. However, people seemed to take the delays with good spirit, as is evidenced in this view outside a refreshment stand at Waterloo on July 31st 1943.*

Right: *Even though delays were inevitable, the railways endeavoured to keep their passengers informed of what was happening. The impersonality of loud-speaker announcements, when services, platform departures and arrival times were continually changing, led to the introduction of information men. The service seemed somehow more personal, more human, as is shown in this view of a London Transport 'Information Man' sparing a few moments for an injured seaman in the bustle at Liverpool Street in November 1940.*

often occupied the best part of 24 hours – with many passengers standing all the way.

Perhaps the worst incident of over-crowding is recorded at Kettering where a woman travelling by train had been taken ill and died; before her body could be removed and the train allowed to progress, 95 people had to be asked by the station-master to get off the train.

Scheduled services were frequently delayed as a priority troop train went through; while in some cases regular passenger trains were simply taken over by the Military Transport Liaison Officers, and the passengers turned out (often at a remote station where only the most basic facilities existed). However, the biggest problem of all was, quite simply

that the stock and locomotives were very often not quite where they should be. This had a multiplying effect; so that even if a service had a clear line to its destination, it could end up being several hours late arriving there, because the train allocated for that journey was still working on another service which had been delayed. When delayed trains finally did arrive, they would often have missed their 'path', and in turn be forced to wait for a clear road. This was overcome wherever possible, with station staff going to extreme lengths to secure an alternative train, even if it was nowhere near adequate for the numbers wishing to travel. In due course, the problem was partially resolved when the Railway Executive introduced a form of coach

pooling which involved almost all of the 46,000 coaches in service.

Above: *If any picture ever told a story, this view at Euston on January 29th 1940 says it all. The atrocious weather of the winter of 1939/40 created numerous problems all over the railway network. A milder spell in mid-January compounded these, when the effects of snow and ice were added to by intense fog which blanketed the whole country. Coupled with the other problems of operating a transport system in wartime, the delays were somewhat inevitable. The chalked slogan on the bottom of the board, reads 'SCOTCH 'UP' TRAINS RUNNING APPROX. 350 MINUTES LATE'.*

Keeping them running

As discussed earlier, the state of Britain's railways in 1938 was one in which the 'Big Four' could take some pride. Their investment programmes in the pre-war years had seen a number of the pre-grouping locomotive classes disappear entirely, with others ready to be phased out. A variety of modernisation programmes in full swing saw new designs in motive power, providing fast streamlined locomotives, workmanlike shunting engines and powerful mixed traffic types. In the early years of the war, the building programme continued with 170 new locomotives entering service in the first six months. Against this 135 were withdrawn, with about 20% of these being scrapped, though in the same six month period 157 locomotives which had been 'in store' or condemned were repaired and returned to work.

Therefore the percentage of new or repaired locomotives was quite high when the number of machines in service peaked at 19,625 in 1942. However the daily toll of high running, limited parts, indifferent coal, and less than desirable maintenance schedules began to take a toll. The loss of skilled workers, replaced by callow apprentices and women, also took its toll until the time they became fully trained. Whilst everyone worked to their maximum, it was not sufficient, and inevitably the machines took the toll. However, a re-build, overhaul, or major service at the works was a luxury denied to many engines. Instead the lot fell on the loco's home shed, where hasty patched jobs were effected in less than ideal surroundings. Foreign engines which failed at a depot were repaired, but generally it was a 'make-do and mend job', barely sufficient to get the locomotive off their hands and back home.

As the war progressed the situation worsened, with depots in the invasion build-up zone (ie mainly the Southern Railway) bearing the brunt of the work. Shed personnel worked hard to turn round failed locomotives, but according to one retired shed superintendent, 'it was always an uphill job, with three locos waiting to take the place of the one you'd repaired'. The volume of work put into maintenance during this period testifies to a superhuman effort, which will never again be repeated on Britain's railways. Hours were extended, with 14 hour days becoming commonplace. For footplate crews this was probably followed by a few snatched hours in distant lodgings if they were lucky. More commonly, a cold empty railway carriage was their lot, unless an accommodating guard would let them rest in front of his stove for an hour or so.

Coupled with this, the vagaries of the British weather had to be contended with, and during the very first winter of the war which turned out to be a major freeze-up, numerous problems were encountered. In the north fog and snow all but brought some routes to a halt, whilst in the south

severe frost resulted in arcing on some of the 3rd-rail electrified systems. Shortages of materials for both running and permanent way departments affected the repairs needed, but always the resources were found just at the last moment. Track was swapped from minor lines and placed on main lines, whilst sleepers from closed lines were cleaned up and re-used in sidings.

Finally, mention should be made of the inter-company transfers which also affected the efficiency of the service. Locomotives were loaned between the companies, with the GWR borrowing large numbers during the early years of the war to replace those 0-6-0s which had been requisitioned by the War Department. To men at sheds in South Wales, Lancashire & Yorkshire Railway or LNWR design tank engines were an unknown quantity and despite very earnest efforts to keep the engines in good order they regularly failed. When it eventually arrived home to its northern shed choice words would be expressed at the abilities of 'foreigners'.

Opposite: *Gresley LNER Class N2 0-6-2T, No 4559, seen shunting in the darkness of a London goods yard in November 1943. Working by the dim light of a shaded lamp, the crews check destination labels, an awkward and difficult task, particularly on rain swept nights.*

Top Left: *As Britain prepared for the invasion of France in 1944, locomotives and crews were worked almost to breaking point. After a few hours respite, the crew of this unidentified LMS Royal Scot 4-6-0 fill tender No 9335 with water at Camden Shed to top up the 4,000 gallons carried by these machines.*

Top Right: *With sunlight filtering through a crack in the shed roof, a re-tubing operation takes place on March 14th 1944, as the build-up to the invasion extends the daily toil.*

Bottom Left: *When this picture of a tired fireman was discovered, there was no information to accompany it . . . but was anything else needed?*

Bottom Right: *When there was no room under cover, engines had to be repaired where they stood as was the case for this fitter and his mate, working on a jammed outside cylinder.*

Women at work

In 1938 around 26,000 women were employed on the railways. Their jobs fell mainly into two categories, clerical and domestic staff: clerks, typists, telephone/telegraph operators, cooks, mess-room attendants, refreshment room staff, carriage cleaners, and crossing keepers. However, by and large it was a male dominated industry, with 650,000 men on the combined payrolls.

At the outbreak of war, it was perhaps understandable that many men wished to enlist in the armed forces. At first only a few were released for war service, including those who were in one of the military reserve forces. A large number of men were in fact reservists for the Royal Engineers, and as soon as they could be released, these railway engineers went overseas to help run Britain's military railway service. Eventually around 103,000 railway employees were released from railway service and went away to war.

To combat the general shortage of manpower, the Ministry of Labour directed women into work on farms, in factories and on the railways. By 1943, the number of women working on the railway peaked at 105,703, with members of the gentler sex being found in almost every avenue of railway service. Now for the first time, a new term 'Railwaywoman' was heard, as women became porters, 'delivery-men', 'signalmen', 'lampmen', station announcers and booking clerks. In addition to these 'light' duties, women were also found at work on much more manual tasks: loading goods trains, oiling and greasing, working on the permanent way staff, driving delivery vans, or at the sheds as loco cleaners and fire-raisers.

On the work-benches, at the sheds and in the railway workshops, they trained to become engineers. Like the men alongside them, they soon learned to undertake skilled work such as core-making, copper-smithing, welding, turning, joinery, and concrete mixing. After a short period of training these 'railwaywomen' were paid the same rate as men doing comparable work. This was largely on the insistence of the rail unions, who fought a lengthy battle for equality in pay. Consequently,

Opposite: *In peacetime, work for Mrs Phelps was found in a mineral water factory, but in September 1942 she was captured on film as an oiler on the Southern Railway; but however did she manage to walk around a railway yard in those shoes?*

Below Top: *The influx of women into the railway service was slow at first, but as more men in 'non-reserved occupations' were called up, they flooded in. The LPTB was amongst the first to retrain women, as in the case of this former Metropolitan Railway employee who is being trained as a booking clerk at Baker Street Station.*

Below Bottom: *Just a few weeks from D-Day, women were much in evidence at London stations helping soldiers to check if their trains were running. Interestingly, this view at Charing Cross shows the work of the official censor, who has removed the badge from the sergeant's sleeve.*

Right: *Training for ticket clerks took just five weeks in the Southern Railway's school, after which girls were sent to a station for two weeks as a 'learner'. After this they were considered qualified, but were doubtlessly watched by the anxious station masters to whom they were assigned.*

these women were well paid by standards of the day. Many were wives of existing railwaymen, or of railwaymen who had enlisted in the armed forces. Additionally many had families, and still had to care for their homes and children after a long day at work. On analysis, it can be safely said that the maintenance of the British railways was in no small part due to the sterling efforts of these women who by the end of the war made up around one sixth of the total employees in the service.

At the end of the war, the majority of women working on the railways left their temporary employment and resumed their peace-time occupations. Some of those who left, later returned and remained at work on the railways for many years, though normally they were engaged only on light duties or clerical grades. A few managed to find permanent work in the industry that had adopted them when the war ended, however by the time of nationalisation in 1948 it was once more a male dominated industry, with women only accounting for about 9.5% of the total workforce.

Opposite Top Left: *Light duties were not the only railway skills learnt by women in the war, as can be seen by this girl working on re-metalling a bearing at Crewe works.*

Opposite Bottom Left: *The Great Central line was built to London in a period of great social change, but the engineers who installed this point rodding would have scarcely believed that its regular maintenance would fall to Mrs Leighton of Nottingham.*

Opposite Right: *By September 1941, over 2,500 women were working in almost every aspect of railway service, just like Catherine Barrat who formerly worked in the Terry's chocolate works at York. Though as her 'temporary' arm band shows, she transferred to driving a LNER delivery van from the local station.*

Right: *It wasn't just working class women who were directed into the railway service, as can be gathered from this picture in London's West End. Fresh from her success as the leading lady in a local theatre, actress Daphne Goodacre pilots her new 'leading man' in her daytime job with the LMS.*

Freight traffic

General freight traffic for both civilian and military needs was regulated by the Ministry of Supply, and managed by Regional Transport Committees. Zoning of supplies, district by district, was introduced, to make each region self-supporting, and therefore partially independent. There was a noted increase in home-produced food encouraged by the 'Dig For Victory' campaign, which saw the establishment of several hundred new regional agricultural schemes. This reduced the number of freight miles considerably, eliminating needless long-distance cross country trips. However, this was balanced out by an increase in freight for home produced items such as sugar beet, tractors, butter and meat, the bulk of which had previously been imported.

Throughout the war years, Britain was heavily dependent on trans-Atlantic convoys to provide it with the necessities of daily life. The stories of the terrible losses suffered by Britain's Merchant Navy have been well documented elsewhere, so it is sufficient to say that they literally kept Britain alive. Once these convoys had arrived at their ports of destination, the job of forwarding the precious cargoes fell on the British railways. The convoy trains were given an immediate priority over most other forms of freight traffic, primarily in order to get the goods away from the dockland areas, which nightly came under heavy aerial attack. Once the goods were loaded onto their respective trains, they were pulled away to 'safe' marshalling points, from where they would be worked onward in the fullness of time.

Another form of freight traffic which developed, emanated from newly built Government factories in rural areas. These factories were the result of a Ministry of Supply policy to build on green-field sites, close to sources

supplying the raw materials used in production. This was a logical move, because often the raw material was heavy whilst the finished product was light. By this strategy, the demand on railway freight movements were reduced by up to 40%, though movements in workers' trains increased by about 26%.

Civilian traffic which had previously been carried by other means, particularly coast-wise shipping, was now forced on to the railways – specifically coal from North-East England which had plied down the east coast to London. By 1943, around 4 million tons of coal were being carried each week, of which about 45% had been moved by coastal shipping in the pre-war years. To handle this traffic, block trains were introduced to run from collieries to distribution centres. Trains were marshalled, with wagons placed in strict order, in an attempt to reduce the amount of marshalling and shunting involved.

Other types of fuel were essential to the national effort, and the country was heavily dependent on imported oil and petroleum products. Long hazardous

Opposite: *Contrasts in mobile freight in Grove Street, Deptford on March 21st 1940. Southern Railway Class E1, No 2215, running bunker first from WD Supply Reserve Depot, passes the Morris Commercial 'Garment Van' which was supplied new to the Co-op Tailoring Factory in Leeds, and is possibly still in their service despite being so far from home. The shaded head lights, and white bands round lamp standards bear mute witness to the black-out regulations.*

Top Right: *Like the Co-op tailoring, firms like Montague Burton were kept busy throughout the war first supplying uniforms, then 'de-mob' suits. Burton's delivery vans, with their Leeds registration plates soon appeared at a number of distribution points based at stations around the country.*

Bottom Right: *The most unusual loads soon began to appear in station yards, replacing the normal peace-time traffic. Heckmondwike Station on the ex-L&YR line from Mirfield to Bradford was used to seeing loads of coal, or woollen cloth in its goods yard, but this view shows the vast amount of barbed wire traffic which was despatched during the war years.*

journeys made by convoys from the middle-east or America saw billions of barrels of oil arriving at ports along the west coast. At an early stage of the war, a number of pipelines were constructed to convey this fuel to distribution centres located well away from the ports. However, despite this, at least 3,000,000 gallons of oil or petrol still had to be moved daily by the railways.

All of these freight movements came at a time when resources were stretched, with the overriding priority being given to military traffic, troop trains etc. Despite these constraints, and a reduction in staff, the railways continued to get the goods through. A major source of traffic in steel making areas were the 'war salvage'

Above: *Prior to 1939, the LNER operated few boat train services, though it would hardly have envisaged that a request for a 'boat train' for the Ministry of Supply would have looked like this load passing through London in August 1942. The location is classified as 'secret' by the official censor, but could it be on the North Woolwich branch?*

Right: *During the London 'blitz' almost 60% of the city's houses were destroyed or badly damaged. In all about 80% required repair at any one time, and to effect these repairs, supplies of raw materials were brought into the city daily. In September 1941, GWR Class 5700 0-6-0PT No 3727 heads for the city passing near Southall carrying timber for the public works departments.*

trains which brought in every conceivable form of scrap iron available – varying from old bedsteads to the railings from civic parks and stately homes.

The necessities of a country at war saw a nation resorting to some very unusual practices, like the burning of peat, use of seaweed in foodstuffs, and the manufacture of 'timber' from pulped paper or sawdust. In the course of these schemes, it fell to the railways to transport these unusual materials to a variety of destinations. One amusing story from this period is that of a non-refrigerated van, which arrived late one Saturday evening in 1943 at a small County Durham station. When opened, it was found to be carrying several boxes of

Above: *To cater for the growing agricultural traffic, new stations, depots and warehouses were opened all over the country, though at Feltwell Fen in East Anglia, a whole new 20 mile stretch of 'light railway' was opened. The 5,000 acre growing area which had defied farmers for years was reclaimed by the Ministry of Agriculture in under a year. The Wissington Light Railway was formally opened by the Minister of Agriculture, Mr Robert Hudson, on July 14th 1941, who is pictured on the footplate of the Manning Wardle 0-6-0T (works No 2006), which bears the headboard 'Bread & Butter Express'.*

Left: *Whether the job was big or small, the railways handled it, as was the case when a complete farm was re-located from the Home Counties to the West Country following the requisition of the farmer's land for an RAF base. Almost the entire siding and platform space was taken up with loaded vans and wagons, when the farm was moved lock, stock and barrel on March 10th 1941.*

ripe bananas, which would have been rotten by the time they were forwarded to the USAF base they were intended for. Consequently, a village which had seen very little foreign fruit since 1939 engaged in an act of community robbery – with a little connived aid from sympathetic LNER employees!

Military freight was the main source of traffic, the complexity of which would fill a book on its own. Basically there were four main peak periods when military freight was at its height: first being the mobilisation of the BEF in 1939, the second being on the evacuation from Dunkirk the following year. In fact the BEF left almost all of its equipment in France, but in the months following Dunkirk all the repatriated units had to be re-equipped with supplies being brought by rail. The next two periods were times when Britain went on the offensive. In 1942 came the despatch of the 1st Army to North Africa, when almost 700 military freights were run in addition to 150,000 wagon loads conveyed on normal freight services. Then came the greatest period of freight working of all,

the prelude to the D-Day landings of June 1944. This time alone saw thousands of extra military freight workings, most of which headed for the military concentration depots which had been created all over the southern counties in the latter part of 1943. Complete goods yards, some capable of holding 2,500 wagons, were constructed on sites where only the barest railway service existed before. From these new yards, vast quantities of stores were eventually shipped out to France: Micheldever depot near Winchester (nicknamed 'Woolworths'), boasted it could supply anything from nuts and bolts to a complete engine for a tank.

Opposite Left: *Dried food became a staple part of the British diet during the war years, with dried milk and powdered egg being the most used. Naturally, it fell to the Railways to move these loads quickly away from their ports of import, but they had to maintain a very strict level of security as there was quite a 'black-market' demand for these goods. On the ration, this dried milk from America and New Zealand sold for around 9d (4p) a can.*

Opposite Right: *With food and consumer goods in such short supply, it seems strange that this load discovered at Euston station in December 1943, went unclaimed. Turkeys, 60 denier stockings and oranges, all worth a king's ransom are being examined by LMS staff, who were probably just part of a small stream of people who would come and stare at these precious items.*

Top Right: *Coal, ever important, was literally Britain's life-blood in the war, and miners were then looked on as heroes. They literally kept the home fires burning, but this unidentified group could still pose for the Camera in January 1943, amidst a crowded yard of coal wagons awaiting despatch.*

Bottom Right: *Imports of oil and petroleum were essential for the vehicles used by both the military and civilians. This precious cargo moved day and night, and even over Christmas 1943 the traffic continued as this view of Cambridge shows: a lengthy train of 'road spirit' tanks passing a local headed by LNER (ex-Great Eastern) F3 2-4-2T No 8075, with a crowded goods yard and shed in the background.*

Refreshments

In the pre-war years, rail catering services were at their zenith; trains like the Cornish Riviera Express, Yorkshire Pullman, Coronation Scot, and Golden Arrow represented the last word in passenger luxury. In September 1939, there were almost 900 restaurant cars in regular daily service, with countless station hotels, buffets, dining rooms and the like. However, on the outbreak of war, these services virtually disappeared overnight. The first casualty was the immediate withdrawal of almost all the restaurant cars, whilst at station buffets and hotels, what little food that remained on sale was just the most basic fare.

Within a few months 'Sorry No . . .' notices began to appear. Crockery and cutlery became scarce; in consequence, spoons chained to buffet counters became a common sight. Curious looking sugar was spooned into cracked cups containing a variety of indifferent liquids which respectively passed as tea, coffee, and

Above: *When the Railway executive withdrew buffet and dining cars in September 1939, it also classified stewards who worked in them as available for military service. Consequently, as these services were gradually reintroduced, women had to be employed in their place. In this LNER buffet car, on May 19th 1941, a female 'Steward' draws a drink for servicemen bound for Norwich.*

Right: *To cater for servicemen travelling long-distance, a new form of rail catering was introduced on January 20th 1941. For the first time, travelling canteens were introduced, having been designed to be carried in coach compartments. The meals which cost 10 (old) pence are seen here being officially introduced by Princess Helena Victoria, Colonel Moore-Brabazon (Minister of Transport) and Lord Stamp.*

cocoa. Members of the forces were somewhat better served, usually in special canteens, staffed largely by middle-aged ladies in various uniforms, denoting their membership of the WVS, Red Cross etc.

These canteens were opened whenever a troop train was expected, even in the dead of night, though at some busy stations the canteens were continuously staffed 24 hours a day.

Packed lunch boxes were prepared for both civilian and military passengers, whilst on certain trains restaurant cars were re-introduced from 1940 onwards. Towards the end of the war, a better variety of food was becoming available, and the railway companies made an impressive effort to resume catering standards, despite the rationing of food which still continued. An example of this was the Southern Railway which introduced 12 'Station Maid' tea trollies. Jointly designed by the Southern and the Empire Tea Bureau, these attractive looking carts plied the platforms of the main Southern stations, taking food to hungry passengers. Even 'cream' cakes, which were now beginning to appear after an absence of six and a half years, reached

the customer in perfect order – each trolley having a specially-sprung covered cake rack!

Above: *When restaurant cars were withdrawn in 1939, packed lunch boxes were supplied to rail travellers. The leisurely personal service in evidence at Euston on September 13th 1939 is in marked contrast with what followed after the 'phoney war' period.*

Left: *The post-war tea trolley appeared on Southern stations early in 1946 and even though heavy rationing was still in force, it provided a standard of luxury unthought of just a few months earlier. Six foot long by three foot six inches wide, it carried four, 3-gallon insulated tea urns, two ice cream cabinets and was electrically driven. Though who can tell if the cream in the cakes is real or artificial?*

Hospital trains

When the Government took control of the railways by The Railway Executive Committee, one of its earliest priorities, was to repeat a course of action it had undertaken successfully during World War I. Then, a number of Ambulance Trains had been ordered for use at home and overseas. Throughout those war years, these trains had ferried their passengers to hospital or repatriation with their families. Several remained in duty until the early 1920s, with the last one being returned to the LMS a few months after the grouping of 1923.

The success of moving injured military personnel by train having thus proved itself, led to the immediate formation of several ambulance trains in 1939. Again they were developed for use either at home or overseas, with formation and numbers of coaches adjusted accordingly. The trains were fully furnished and

manned by doctors, nurses and ward orderlies. There were wards for both stretcher and sitting cases, with provision to care for mental patients. Kitchens, pharmacies, treatment rooms and even operating theatres were built into the trains. A number of overseas trains were provided with decontamination units, with facilities for disposing of infested clothing, whilst all the trains had the capability to deal with infectious cases. Several vehicles were in fact those constructed for the Great War hospital trains, but the majority were converted coaching stock.

In addition to the ambulance trains, a series of Evacuation Trains were also formed, with 27 having been commissioned by March 1941. These were primarily designed for the evacuation of casualties, carrying them from danger areas to places of safety. They were employed to move hospital patients away from the big cities to cottage hospitals in the countryside, though their conception came from other fears. The threat of gas attacks and mass bombings had convinced the Government that all the major cities in Britain would come under attack, and that the resulting casualty toll would be very high. The primary purpose of the evacuation train was to sit outside the city whilst an attack was in progress, then enter on the 'all clear' to provide an emergency field hospital, which could treat the casualties, and later evacuate them to a place of safety. Fortunately, conditions under which these trains were to be used were not experienced, and because of their value elsewhere a number were made into full ambulance trains or converted for other use.

As with the military freight traffic, use of ambulance and evacuation trains appears to have had specific peaks. These were immediately prior to the evacuation of Dunkirk, following the disastrous raid on Dieppe by Canadian and British Commando forces, after the 'D-Day landings', and in the last months of the war when the final assault was made towards Berlin. In that latter period the trains were not only used to bring home soldiers wounded in the final offensive, but also thousands of emaciated servicemen and civilians who had been liberated from the Nazi concentration camps in Germany, Poland and Austria.

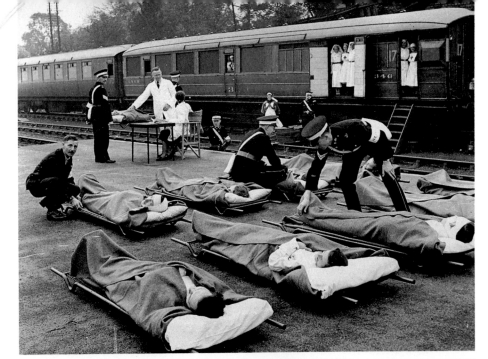

Opposite Top: *The immediate formation of the ambulance trains was handled by the carriage departments of the 'Big Four', with work being carried out as a top priority. Here at Swindon Carriage works, Great Western stock is given the final touches with the painting of 'Geneva' (red) crosses on the roof.*

Opposite Bottom: *By contrast, Ambulance trains supplied by the LNER were furnished with illuminated crosses. This device is being fitted to the roof of an evacuation train on November 24th 1939, as ex-GN Class 02 2-8-0. No 3483 coasts past on an empty van train.*

Top Right: *Two days later the same train officially entered service, and was based on the former GER section. The official commissioning ceremony was accompanied by a demonstration of evacuation techniques using LNER employees as volunteer 'victims'.*

Bottom Right: *One of the 'France' ambulance trains of the British Quartermaster's Unit, at Dover Marine Station on February 7th 1940. The 'Eclipse' sign, complete with cat wearing a bowler hat, boots and spats, originated from the words of a famous army song.*

Luggage

With the tremendous movement of military and civilian personnel during the period 1939-45, another strain was put on the railway networks. Strangely, it is the side of railway operations that is rarely discussed, but one which no railway system would ever operate without – passengers' luggage. Almost every station in the land had facilities for handling luggage, varying from small cupboards at tiny country stations to vast basement rooms extending beneath the main-line termini.

Luggage was basically in two types: personal items carried on the train journey with the passenger, or luggage sent in advance at a much reduced rate. At the outbreak of war Britain's railways were handling around 50 million pieces of

Top: *'Find the porter': King's Cross September 14th 1944, with the left luggage room brimming with a huge collection of prams and bicycles. This huge collection was the result of an unauthorised and large scale return of evacuees, despite the Government's empassioned 'Stay away for the present' warnings.*

Left: *Manchester Central Station on June 23rd 1940, with a Post Office official helping sort a mountain of parcels. Almost the entire mountain is comprised of packages of civilian clothing being returned home by men who have 'joined up' in the armed forces.*

Opposite: *The temporary left luggage cloakroom, established at Fenchurch Street Station, was typical of hundreds of others at stations up and down the country. These depositories differed from normal luggage offices in that they were intended just for members of HM Forces. Here they could leave almost any item of kit, except great coats, for 24 hours free of charge. Weapons could also be checked in, as is exampled by this fresh faced soldier handing over his rifle, without anyone giving it a second glance. The age of the soldiers in the foreground illustrates the age at which young men were expected to fight and even lay down their lives for King and Country: October 22nd 1942.*

advance luggage a year, with an additional 75 million pieces being stored in left luggage offices for periods over 12 hours. At the outbreak of war the 'luggage in advance' service was withdrawn, though passengers could still send on trunks, suitcases etc by the standard luggage service. Unfortunately no statistics appear to have been kept for the period of the war years, but it is conceivable that even with the restrictions the figures shown above would have doubled or even trebled.

One form of luggage which became a common site at the stations during the early months of the war, were the 'civvies': clothes and personal effects which were being sent home by men enlisting in the forces. Inside a few months the standard issue, navy, and air-force blue kit bags began to appear in their stead, as servicemen moved around the country carrying their essential belongings with them.

In fact the kit bag became synonymous with railway travel; for it also doubled as something to sit on in coaches where all the seats were taken, or on crowded platforms where men had to wait for trains which could be running up to several hours late. To avoid congestion on passenger trains, certain restrictions were imposed to regulate the amount of luggage which could be carried by each person. Inevitably these rules failed, because guards turned a 'blind eye', or because people were unwilling to send luggage ahead unaccompanied (when it might easily be lost for days on end). Eventually the problem was in part resolved by the coupling of a passenger-rated goods van to many passenger trains.

Armament traffic

The movement of military traffic during the war years was both intensive, and of course highly classified. Even with the freedom of information now afforded fifty years on, full details are difficult to find. Therefore only a generalisation can be made concerning this traffic, whose full details if available would probably fill an entire book. The size, scope and variety of military traffic during the war years can only be hinted at though the accompanying selection of photographs which only show part of the diversity of military loads carried on Britain's railways. The vast majority of loads went 'under wraps', and in many instances with even the locomotive crews not knowing what they were carrying.

Some consignments were impossible to conceal inside goods vans or under wagon sheets, so larger items were often crated or loaded in packing cases. Where this was not possible, the loads would often be disguised, or their appearance altered in some respects in order to confuse any information which might be gained by the enemy, either through aerial reconnaissance or from their agents in Britain.

Above: *Twelve inch naval guns, bound for shipyards on the Clyde, are seen leaving for the north on specially designed LNER wagons on May 10th 1944, as Britain prepares to open 'the second front'.*

Below: *A number of freight-concentration depots were opened at strategic locations in the south of England. When the Allies were ready to invade France, it would* need its own railway system, and this picture taken on February 23rd 1944, shows one of the biggest 'train sets' of all time. Everything that would be needed for operating a railway in France, locomotives, coaches, weapons, hospital trains, and even refrigerated food vans, were assembled for shipping in pre-fabricated kit form.

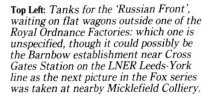

Top Left: *Tanks for the 'Russian Front', waiting on flat wagons outside one of the Royal Ordnance Factories: which one is unspecified, though it could possibly be the Barnbow establishment near Cross Gates Station on the LNER Leeds-York line as the next picture in the Fox series was taken at nearby Micklefield Colliery.*

Bottom Left: *Instantly recognisable, the LMS carriage and wagon works, Derby, with one of the biggest orders ever out-shopped. This train of eight, 12-inch rail mounted howitzers was just one of the 'secret' orders produced by the 44,000 employees in LMS workshops around the country. December 12th 1944.*

Bottom Right: *Cleckheaton Junction, at Mirfield on the ex-LYR 'Spen Valley' line, with the main trans-Pennine line to Leeds in the background. A secret load of crated supplies for Russia on March 3rd 1942, is held whilst yard-men check wagon ropes. From the stencilled identification numbers on each packing case, the crates would seem to be holding 'Bren Gun Carriers' and would probably have originated from either Huddersfield, Sheffield or Penistone.*

Accidents

Despite the intensity of traffic movements, the war years were relatively accident free. Several incidents occurred as a result of bomb damage to tracks and stations, but these are not officially recorded as accidents. Of those true railway accidents which did occur, the following were among the most serious. Shortly after the outbreak of war, a rear-end collision occurred near Bletchley on October 13th 1939 when the 7.50 Euston to Stranraer ran into the back of the 7.37 Euston to Inverness. The following March a more traditional type of accident happened between Aviemore and Carr Bridge, when the failure of a drawbar resulted in 21 wagons and brake-van running away backwards and colliding with a Perth-Inverness freight killing the driver and fireman.

An unusual event took place at Wembley Central in October 1940, when a station barrow being taken down a ramp ran away and became wedged on the running line. It was struck by the 11.50am Liverpool-Euston express, which was de-railed with a number of passengers killed and about 50 injured. A few weeks later, on November 4th 1940, one of the most serious rail accidents of the war occurred at Norton Fitzwarren on the GWR. A driver on a Paddington-Penzance train misread the signals and ran into trap points, leaving 26 dead and 56 injured.

At Harold Wood on February 10th 1941, the driver of a Liverpool Street-Southend passenger train ran into the rear of the preceding express to Norwich. Four months later a head on collision resulted when a Plymouth-Paddington express met a west-bound freight on the same section of track near Slough on July 2nd. This was followed by a side to side collision at Eccles on December 8th, when the Rochdale-Pennington local service over-ran signals after the premature suspension of 'fog working', and collided with another local passenger train from Kenyon to Manchester.

In 1942 two major accidents occurred, the first being at Beighton on the former Great Central line, when a troop train struck a misplaced load on a freight train.

A load of steel sheet had slipped so badly that it was out of gauge, and fouling the opposite running line, the resulting collision claimed the lives of 16 servicemen. On November 13th at Appleford, near Didcot on the GWR, the midnight Paddington to Birkenhead ran into several derailed wagons from a goods train, claiming the lives of four people aboard the express. The following year seems remarkably accident free, with the only major accident reported, caused by the collapse of a locomotive firebox at Honeybourne near Worcester. It involved a USA 2-8-0, allocated to the GWR:

The final year of the war, when traffic was at its height, was relatively free from major accidents; though one occurred at Esher on January 28th 1945, when an electric train from Waterloo to Portsmouth collided with a steam hauled train to Bournemouth due to a signalman's error.

Though not a frequent occurrence, it was quite common for sparks from locomotive chimneys to set fire to combustible material in open wagons they were hauling. When these wagons contained explosives the situation was critical, though despite the amount of military traffic carried between 1939 and 1945, only three accidents stand out in their severity when the trains involved literally blew themselves up. The first happened on June 2nd 1944 when a wagon behind a WD 2-8-0 No 7337 carrying bombs for the USAF caught fire at Soham, Cambridgeshire. The crew did all they could to avert the destruction of the town though the fireman, and the local signalman were both killed and the station raised to the ground. A similar incident occurred nine months later, when a LMS 0-6-0 4F carrying a load of sea mines to Carnforth caught fire at Bootle in Cumbria, the resulting explosion killed the driver and injured the fireman and the guard. The third accident occurred just three weeks later near Selby in Yorkshire when a number of 500lb bombs exploded, though this time it was the driver of a passing train who was killed. In each of these instances, when the crews discovered the fire, they made courageous efforts to uncouple the blazing wagon from the rest of the train, thus reducing the danger of the whole train exploding.

Opposite Top: *Five people, including three sailors going home on leave from the naval base at Plymouth, were killed when the 6.20pm express to Paddington crashed near Slough. Unfortunately, the express' progress was impeded when it collided head on with a goods train on the same section of track. Of particular interest is the Military Liaison Officer standing in the foreground surveying the urgent work of clearing the main line.*

Opposite Bottom: *Almost total devastation, caused not by a bomb or the result of enemy action, but by the simple, though tragic, case of a station barrow running away and fouling the running line: the aftermath is seen at Wembley Central on October 13th 1940, with LMS Patriot Class 5XP 4-6-0 No 5529, completely over on one side, with its 3,500 gall Fowler tender No 4495, at right angles to the cab. In the background, the shattered remains of a parachute water tank which once stood at the end of the platform are seen in front of a 'pooled' wagon which had formerly belonged to Dundee Corporation.*

Below: *In complete contrast to the cover picture, LNER Class B12 4-6-0 No 8556 lays in a sorry dejected state after being involved in a collision near Brentwood. The accident occurred in February 1941, when a Liverpool Street-Southend train crashed into the back of a stationary Liverpool Street-Norwich express.*

Locos for abroad

Initially the immediate needs of the WD were met by commandeering locomotives from the 'Big Four', with 0-6-0 types being particularly popular. However, many of the 2-8-0 ex-ROD locomotives (to a former Great Central Railway design) from the First World War, which were still giving sterling service on some main line railways were initially refused by the Ministry when offered to them, though a few later saw service in the middle-East. Instead the WD resorted to ordering new machines for service in France. In the following months, the Ministry of Supply placed orders for 240, 2-8-0s to the Stanier 8F design modified with air brake equipment for overseas use. Two orders for 100 locomotives were placed respectively with Beyer Peacock, and the North British Loco Co, whilst the remaining 40 were ordered from the Vulcan Foundry.

Meanwhile the requisitioned locos were shipped out to the continent through Harwich, Hull and Felixstowe. Several of the ex-GWR Dean Goods 0-6-0s passed through Ipswich in November 1939, painted in a dull-black livery with pale yellow 'WD' lettering. Unfortunately, the BEF was forced to retreat from France before most of the new locos could be

delivered, these were then re-assigned for use in other theatres of war.

Further batches of the Stanier design were ordered throughout the war for use in Britain, with members of the class being built by all four British companies. Most were given the LMS markings of their designing company, but some were regarded as LNER stock and marked accordingly.

The supply of standard British designs to countries as diverse as Turkey and Egypt may seem strange, when compared with what was happening elsewhere on Britain's railways. On the Great Western, shortages of motive power were creating considerable problems, and in turn Britain had to seek overseas aid in order to keep its railways running. So on December 11th 1942, the whistle of an American locomotive was heard when the first main line steam engine was handed over at Paddington Station. Though these engines were actually intended for use overseas, a number of them began handling traffic which had previously been in the charge of British locos now working abroad. After the war a number of American 0-6-0Ts were taken in to British stock, and many remained in service almost to the end of steam on the Southern Region.

In 1943, the Ministry of Supply's own machines ('utility' engines built to a design by R A Riddles) began to appear.

There were two major types: a 2-8-0 with 4ft 8in driving wheels, and a tractive effort of 34,215lbs; and a somewhat similar but less numerous 2-10-0 type of almost identical power but which, at 78 tons 6cwt, weighed 8 tons 1cwt more than the 2-8-0s. Additionally a powerful 0-6-0ST was designed, primarily for work as a shunting engine. These locomotives

were also sent to a variety of countries overseas, as well as being put into service in Britain. After the war large numbers were shipped back to Britain, and put into store before eventually being taken over by the newly nationalised British Railways in 1948, with 733 2-8-0 and 25 2-10-0s entering service to replace many of the prematurely worn-out members of the British fleet.

Opposite Top: *In addition to the engines ordered by the Ministry of Supply to the Stanier 8F design, a number of LMS machines were requisitioned for service in Persia for the supply route to Russia. On November 13th 1941, No 8031 is seen at Crewe whilst being modified for overseas service. The buffer beam is being altered, but the largest modification of all is the conversion to oil burning.*

Opposite Below: *Having been modified the engines stand in ex-works condition awaiting trans-shipment by hazardous convoy routes to their destination. This would see a number of the class being lost below the sea, including four which were aboard the SS* Pentridge Hall *sunk in June 1942. These powerful locos weighed in at 72 tons 5cwt when introduced by Stanier in 1935, however these machines had increased in weight by 4½ tons by their conversion. However, at the same time the tractive effort was reduced from 32,440lb to 31,955lbs.*

Top Right: *WD locomotives to the design by R A Riddles wait to be shipped to the continent on March 13th 1945; the majority appear to be 2-8-0 machines. Alongside stand a number of 55 ton 10cwt tenders, already loaded with coal. Also in the same shipment, but not in this view were a number of Ministry of Supply 0-6-0STs which were also constructed to Riddles' design.*

Bottom Right: *Whilst British workshops were turning out machines for use overseas, Britain was importing locomotives from America. As part of a publicity exercise the first of these 'freight' engines was handed over in an official ceremony at Paddington on December 11th 1942. Colonel Ryan, Chief of Transportation for the American Army, is seen here pointing out some of the unusual features to Lord Leathers and Major General J C H Lee.*

The railway works

In the preceding chapters, mention has been made about locomotive sheds being forced to carry out repairs and overhauls that would by rights have been carried out at the works. The reason for this was two-fold: firstly the necessity to keep engines in service at their home sheds, but mainly due to the reduced capacity of the works themselves.

This reduction in capacity was again brought about for two reasons: one that the works were busy constructing WD locomotives for use overseas, the other that the works were being directed to construct other items for the war effort. This situation applied equally at the private railway contractors, as it did in the workshops of the 'Big Four' companies. Firms like the North British found themselves manufacturing bomb casings, whilst another was ordered to construct naval life-boats.

One reason for the direction of capacity at the workshops was a result of their technical excellence. The works were amongst the finest heavy engineering shops in the country, and in terms of quality and skill they were unrivalled, facets which were vital for a nation struggling to maintain its independence.

The work directed to railway workshops was of the widest variety, as is testified by the entry from the order book of Cowans Sheldon in June 1940. Machine six rafts (Admiralty); Machine four screws; Construct two O/head Cranes

Above: *One of the light armoured personnel carriers manufactured at four railway workshops in Britain: two in Scotland and two in England. Based on a Canadian Army design, these fast moving, semi-amphibious machines were maufactured in large numbers during 1941-2, and were used in both Europe and North Africa.*

Below: *Britain's railway workshops turned out some amazing pieces of engineering during the war years, but none would have been as strange as this walking bridge. These 'unit construction bridges' were supplied to the Royal Engineers who used them to replace conventional bridges destroyed by the retreating enemy. One feature of this December 1944 view is the barrage balloon in the distant sky.*

(Admiralty – Singapore); Construct four, 1 Ton Capstans (Air Ministry); 400 Cupola Covers to be machined (Vauxhall Motors); Machine sample buffer cylinder (Ministry of Supply); machine 4,000 Screwed Bases (David Brown & Sons); Repair two coal hoists (LNER); construct 25ton floating crane (Admiralty, Newcastle); Press and assemble 250 Mortar containers (Ministry of War, India Office).

The above is just a random sample of one week at just one works, but the same story must have been repeated all around the country, with the work-load being spread to as many different centres as possible. In adopting this technique, the Ministries of War and Supply avoided 'putting all their eggs in one basket', and production was kept up, even if one factory was put out of action by a bomb attack. So throughout the war years, railway workshops were kept busy constructing bailey bridges, floating docks, tanks, munitions, aircraft, naval vessels, and a whole host of other machined components. However, locomotive building was not overlooked, and throughout the war, engines for use at home and overseas were turned out in their hundreds.

Above: *Despite the diversity of work being undertaken in the railway workshops, it was still 'business as usual' as new machines were outshopped. A feature of the war years was the continuing appearance of members of the LMS 'Coronation' Class. June 27th 1940,* King George VI *receives finishing touches before the naming ceremony.*

Left: *Not only were young boys and women employed in the railway workshops, but skilled engineers past the age of retirement went back to work – some as old as 80. Mr Sylth, seen at work on bomb casings in a north London railway works, had previously applied his engineering skills as a jeweller and watchmaker.*

Right: *The training of some women as engineers was easier than others, those who had formerly worked as dress-makers and machinists seemed to adapt quicker than those who had worked in other professions. On June 15th 1940, a woman pupil receives instruction before going on to work at a north London loco depot.*

Above: *At the end, after it was all over, there was home. Thousands of returning soldiers passed through Britain's main* line stations on their way to de-mob centres. For this group walking down the sun-lit platform of King's Cross station, *one era has drawn to an end and another is ready to begin.*

Atlantic